*Today is the most wonderful day of my life. I know Italy,
Sicily, Greece and Egypt, and I have never seen anything to
equal the Pena Palace. It's the most beautiful thing I have
ever seen. This is the true Garden of Klingsor, and atop sits
the Castle of the Holy Grail.*

—RICHARD STRAUSS

MARC WALTER

JÉRÔME COIGNARD

DREAM PALACES

The Last Royal Courts of Europe

Preface by
Markus of Habsburg-Lorraine
Archduke of Austria

THE VENDOME PRESS

CONTENTS

OPPOSITE: A photograph of the royal family of Portugal taken at Porto in 1887. Seated in the first row: Queen Maria Pia with Prince Dom Luis Felipe, Princess Amelia, and King Dom Luis I (National Palace of Ajuda, Lisbon).

PRECEDING PAGES: A tower of Pena Palace (page 1); at Stolzenfels, the entrance to the queen's parlor, photographed from her dressing room (page 2); in the Pena Palace park, exotic vegetation and treelike ferns surround the lake (pages 4–5).

OVERLEAF: On the Russian empress's desk at Alexandria Cottage at Peterhof, a small statue of Friedrich Wilhelm III, king of Prussia, her father, figures among the monarch's objects.

On his desk at Kaiservilla, a
photograph of Emperor Franz
Joseph dating from the 1850's.

The freedom to flee official palaces, to escape, for several precious moments, from the constraints of fastidious 11
court ceremony . . . this dream of royal and imperial families was certainly born with the very beginnings of
court life and its stifling etiquette and codified rituals. In the nineteenth century, members of dynastic families could not avoid the rules, and their desire to seek refuge was made even more pressing by the growth of
large capital cities. This is the reason why architects and builders strove to create new living quarters, with an
intimate atmosphere favorable to a more relaxed way of life; more than ever, the idea of private life was at the
forefront.

Far from the overwhelming splendor of St. Petersburg's Winter Palace, Tsar Nicholas I built the cottage on
the Alexandria property as a gift for his wife. And far from the gilded rows of corridors in the Schönbrunn
and Hofburg palaces, Emperor Franz Joseph outfitted Kaiservilla in the town of Bad Ischl, at the foot of the
mountains. It was blissful to be in the park, on the island, at the riverside, enjoying a delightful landscape with
an intimate circle of friends, a few faithful servants, and favorite dogs. Savoring the simple life surrounded by
family, partaking in hunting, jaunts in the woods, trips to the mountains or to a neighboring lake, listening
to music, and playing golf, all made conducting the affairs of state easier to bear.

The decor, furnishings, and accessories of daily life inspired by past centuries, bore witness to the Romantic
spirit, all the while retaining the comfort and convenience of modern life. Certainly starting with the last half of
the nineteenth century, special trains, sumptuously appointed, transported monarchs to their vacation spots. But
trips in carriages, on horseback, or in a surrey were still regarded as amusing pastimes.

Country residences readily took their inspiration from the English cottage or the Palladian[1] villa. But, hun-
gry for chivalric stories and legends, the Romantic era was not content merely to nostalgically recreate a
mythic model such as the medieval fortress.

While in his little "kingdom" in the *Vallée aux Loups*,[2] Chateaubriand dreamed of towers and crenellated
walls, while crowned heads were taking possession of this revivalist style. With the considerable means that
power confers, their whims took on extraordinary forms. The Neuschwanstein Castle remains the most spectacular example, the most moving perhaps, of a refuge meant to invoke a way of life long gone.

With this book, the reader will be afforded an intimate look at Romantic palaces and dwellings, the final
vestiges of a world that technical progress and societal evolution would eventually relegate forever to the
kingdom of lost illusions.[3]

"I had a dream: the wall of centuries appeared to me

It was living flesh made of raw granite

An immobility made from anxiety

An edifice having a noise of multitudes

Of black holes starred by wild eyes, . . .

Huge bas reliefs, colossal frescoes."

—VICTOR HUGO

"Ludwig of Bavaria is a real king, but he presides only over himself and his dreams," wrote Gabriele D'Annunzio. The princes and other monarchs who built castles and palaces were certainly rulers of their dreams, even if some of them also reigned over vast empires. These whimsical dwellings, built during the nineteenth century and up until the dawn of the World War I, belong to the Industrial Age. They are contemporaneous with train trips and long excursions by steamboat. They were born at the same time as the great metal halls and bridges thrust vertiginously upward by engineers confident in their ability. They grew in the shadows of the World's Fairs in London, Paris, Vienna, or Brussels that brought wonders from the world over. They knew the pale flame of gaslight, the delight of central heating, and even the dazzle of electricity. Some of them secretly adopted the latest marvels of contemporary techniques: at Pierrefonds, it was an audacious metal framework; at Kaiservilla in Bad Ischl, it was the early installation of electricity; at Neuschwanstein, it was the use of a steam machine to hoist construction materials up to the summit of a rocky peak. And everywhere, there was the comfort of running water, and modern and invisible heating furnaces. But if these palaces were indeed the "children of the century"[4] their real parents were the historical dramas of Goëthe and Schiller, the novels of Sir Walter Scott, of Bulwer Lytton and Jules Verne, and the operas of Giacomo Meyerbeer and Richard Wagner. They are the last fortresses of Romanticism. Heroic dreams of stone and marble, they seem to be sublime refuges from the new religion of the Industrial Age, from the social ferment swept along by the smoke of its factories. They are immense mirrors trying to capture in their silvered depths a consoling reflection from a bygone era, a lost time[5] that the great destruction of the French Revolution had raised to the glorious level of myth.

These are the "Roman Castles" whose vast corridors one visits as he devours the pages of a book, in search of foreign episodes, of dramas muffled in velvet curtains, of the clinking of blades in hidden corridors. Beneath these colonnades, in the guardrooms, in these antechambers darkened with paneling, who would be astonished to encounter the heroes of "The Last Days of Pompeii" or Knight Goetz de Berlichingen, to hear the silken swish of hoopskirts belonging to ladies in Henry III's court? These dwellings are born from a giddiness of a past that hides itself and is trying to come back to life. Just as at the opera, where, in a once famous scene from *Robert le Diable* (1831), the nuns come out of their tombs and dance in the ruins of an ancient abbey bathed in the worrisome brightness of the moon,[6] these dwellings are born of fantasy visions. They are the fruit of a pact with a modern devil, architect, engineer, or designer. Just as Mephistopheles conjured the apparition of Marguerite before a stunned Faust,[7] the modern devil caused pinnacles, turrets, central towers, drawbridges, pediments, and colonnades to emerge from the earth.

This vision is the luxurious and refined—in a word, habitable—version of the famous "Wall of Centuries" dreamed of by Victor Hugo, a funereal apparition where porphyry and marble, the sword of justice and armor, all gleam together. A bygone era, created in the image of a human epic, now destroyed. These buildings born of an imperial whim retie the knots of this frayed epic in a bourgeois century that was shaking off revolutions and imbued with Positivism.[8]

This refashioned past took on very diverse faces. Sometimes it was Pompeii reborn in the glory of white marble and paintings with red backgrounds; other times it was Byzantium and its mosaics with metal reflections, or else the German Renaissance and Elizabethan England, with motifs in *repoussé* leather. There were also gold tones of baroque Rome, linked to the red velvet in a throne room. China, Turkey, and Moorish Spain were also called forth, punctuating this Romanesque exploration of the "Légende des Siecles"[9] with an exotic "Invitation au voyage."[10]

Favorable to the dreams of knights, Gothic architecture underwent countless metamorphoses. There was the fanciful Gothic of falsely humble "cottages," with trompe l'oeil paintings, and paneling imitating whimsical striated stone. There was the poetic Gothic, Karl Friedrich Schinkel's minimalist and purebred style, which came out of the ruins of old fortified castles on the Rhine. There was the powerful Gothic that triumphed at Pierrefonds, wiping out the archaeological trail with a dizzying verve, and worthy of the "ymagiers" (embellishers) of our cathedrals. Finally, there was the whimsical Gothic, topped by fake central towers, barbed arrows, and fantasy walls that protect nothing. It is theatric Gothic; a painted canvas transposed into granite and slate, halfway between the illuminations in the *Très Riches Heures du duc de Berry*[11] and the naive stacking up of Disneyland. It stretches toward the clouds in the midst of rocky forms torn apart by chasms, where pine trees, appearing almost black, spread out.

As much pipe dreams as "building castles in the air,"[12] but incarnate in stone and mortar, these palaces were intended as "creations" to hold back time, but instead became the things of dreams. Theaters of absence, they are inhabited by the memory of fallen monarchies. Here, friendly phantoms lightly brush past us, as does that of Queen Elizabeth of Romania, the tall and beautiful woman "dressed in long white robes, hair flowing in the wind or covered by a veil, a priestess with pince-nez for myopia," as Paul Morand saw her. Other phantoms wear the tragic mask of a violent death, like Maximilian of Habsburg, dead in Mexico, shot as a common traitor for having dreamed of rebuilding the empire of his ancestor Charles V, or Elizabeth of Austria, stabbed by an anarchist seeking to destroy a crowned head, no matter which one. But for a long time, "Sissi" has been nothing more than her own self-created phantom entirely giving up her inconsolable grief to the solitude of long sea voyages. During one of her countless flights, Emperor Franz Joseph wrote her this note: "My adored angel, I thought I saw your white parasol on the balcony and it brought tears to my eyes." On a sunny afternoon, in Corfu or Bad Ischl, the white parasol of the adored angel still sometimes appears to a casual stroller smitten by love.

PETERHOF

ALEXANDRIA COTTAGE

Tsar Nicholas I of Russia

Tsarina Alexandra Feodorovna of Russia;

née Princess Charlotte of Hohenzollern

Compared to Gatchina, a dark castle with six hundred rooms and three throne rooms, where the future Tsar Nicholas I spent his childhood, or compared to Peterhof Palace, the Russian Versailles and summer residence of the court, Alexandria Cottage looks like a humble abode. It resembles one of the huts that children build with branches in the garden of the "big house." It so happened that this "folly" came into flower at the threshold of the garden of the immense Peterhof Park. This was the palace of Peter I, enlarged by Bartolommeo Francesco Rastrelli in the middle of the eighteenth century and from then on named the Grand Palace to distinguish it from the smaller edifices of Marly Palace, the Hermitage Pavilion, and Monplaisir Palace surrounding it. Facing the sea, on the shores of the Gulf of Finland, it is a grandiose site. On a clear day, it affords views of the mouth of the Neva, at the point where it separates before emptying into the sea. From this vantage point, the tsar could gaze at Kotline Island in front of Kronstadt, where the imperial flotilla used to anchor. By night he could see the lights of St. Petersburg.

The Alexandria estate is on the Baltic shore, southeast of Peterhof's lower park. In the eighteenth century, this land belonged to Prince Alexander Menchikov, who, after a brilliant military career, was promoted to advisor of Catherine I. He would later end his days in exile in Siberia. The site subsequently became a royal hunting ground, although at the end of the century, no one hunted there anymore and herds of deer grew and multiplied undisturbed. In 1825, Tsar Alexander I presented the "Deer Park" to his brother Nicholas as a gift on which to build a summer residence; Alexander died soon after. Nicholas I ascended to the throne

in the same year, and in 1826 signed a decree that "on the site of the ruins of Menchikov, a country house or cottage, along with all outbuildings and a park, be built." He presented this estate, from then on baptized Alexandria, to his wife, Alexandra Feodorovna.

Alexandra was a fragile woman, ravishing but also of a frightening pallor. As a child she was called *Weisse Rose*, or White Rose. The period was one of gallantry that evoked troubadours, the knightly spirit of medieval times, and the refinement of courtly love. Her name at the time was Charlotte; she had not yet been Russified as Alexandra. She was the daughter of King Friedrich Wilhelm III of Prussia, a personal friend of Tsar Alexander I. She met Nicholas, the future tsar, for the first time in Berlin on February 22, 1814. She fell in love by chance, which was good because reasons of state had already decided that their union would seal an alliance between the two countries that had fought against Napoleon. Nicholas himself was much in love with his future wife. At the royal palace in Berlin, on October 23, 1815, the engagement dinner brought together, in addition to members of the two families, Prussian Field Marshal Blücher, victor at Waterloo, and Russian Field Marshal Barclay de Tolly, who also played an important role in the French campaign the year before. While awaiting his wedding, Nicholas traveled throughout Russia to complete his princely education. Afterward he went to England. In a memorandum, Count Nesselrode, Russian minister for foreign affairs, warned him that it would be imprudent to consider English democracy "beneath another sky or in another climate."

Built by Adam Menelaws, a Scottish architect, Alexandria Cottage (left) evokes the Tudor style thanks to its gables and picturesque bow windows. The decorations on the walls and ceiling of the grand staircase are painted in trompe l'oeil made in 1828 according to the sketches of Giovanni Battista Scotti.

PAGE 19: The Baltic Sea seen from the park of the Znamenka Palace, which was attached to the Peterhof estate and reserved for guests of the royal family.

MEDALLION (PAGE 18): A miniature painted by Waldemar Hau in 1834 depicts Tsarina Alexandra Feodorovna in her study at the cottage.

The future Nicholas I's good looks and polite manners struck Countess Boigne, who met the young grand duke at the royal Brighton Pavilion when they were both guests of King George II of England. However, she also noted: "I've really never seen a young man so completely deprived of self-confidence as Grand Duke Nicholas; but is it in fact reasonable to require this quality from a prince and the brother of an absolute monarch?" His marriage to Charlotte took place in St. Petersburg on her birthday, July 1, 1817. It was during the ceremony of her conversion to the Orthodox rite in the chapel of the Winter Palace, that Charlotte received the name Alexandra Feodorovna.

The architects Adam Menelaws, Joseph Charlemagne, Andrei Stackenschneider, and Eduard Gahn supervised construction of the buildings on the Alexandria estate. The master gardeners Freidrich Wendelsdorf and Peter Ehrler, who worked extensively to grade and prepare the site, designed the park. Numerous plant varieties were sent from the botanical gardens and from the park at Taurida Palace in St. Petersburg. Others were ordered from Moscow, Hamburg, and even Marseilles.

Running from east to west by a straight opening, Nikolskaya, or Nicolas Avenue, divides the park into a higher section and a lower section at the seaside. Between 1826 and 1829, Adam Menelaws erected the cottage, the little palace disguised as a rustic house, in an out-of-the-way spot. This picturesque building belongs to a genre the British call "an embellished cottage," a rural retreat longing for the modesty of a countryman's lodging, yet

A portrait of Tsar Nicholas I by Jagor Botman, 1849. Feared by his subjects, this absolute monarch was accorded the nickname "Nicholas the Cudgel."

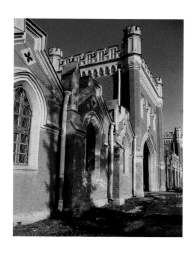

LEFT: The favorite architect of Friedrich Wilhelm III of Prussia, and then of his son, Karl Friedrich Schinkel, erected the neo-Gothic chapel of Saint Alexander Nevski for Nicholas I on the Alexandria estate.

RIGHT: The stables constructed by Adam Menelaws.

adopting certain complicated architectural characteristics for comfort: verandas, a winter garden, corbelled windows crowned by fake merlons.[13] At Tsarkoye Selo, at the edge of Alexander Park, Menelaws created a series of neo-Gothic constructions, and a "retirement house" for horses of the imperial stables, humorously dubbed the Hôtel des Invalides[14] by the monarch's family.

To the eyes of contemporaries, the cottage was Tudor in style. However, the delicate cast iron arcs that decorate its facades owe more to the century of the Industrial Revolution than to the War of the Roses. This decorative whimsy lends its tone to the interior, where the spectacular trompe l'oeil painted on the staircase and in the Naval Study reflects Gothic architecture, and where a fine netting of stucco covers the ceilings in the parlors.

The official presentation of this palace as a gift, as well as its unveiling, took place on July 2, 1829. In December of that year, the cottage received its own coat of arms, decorated with a crown of white roses, a sword, and the motto, "For the faith, the tsar, and the country." The imperial couple took frequent trips there. "I don't like huge things, I rather prefer comfortable, elegant, and smaller places," declared the tsarina. Her noble husband was accustomed to a spartan, unencumbered lifestyle. Even amid the splendor of the Winter Palace at St. Petersburg, his study was simple, and the mattress on his cot was stuffed with hay.

Only the most intimate circle of the imperial family, with their servants, was admitted into this private house, with the exception of July 2, the day after the empress's birthday. On that day, the doors opened wide to the crowd of courtiers. Marquis Adolphe de Custine in his *La Russie en 1839* provides a dazzling account of the celebration, which attracted six thousand carriages, thirty thousand people on foot, and countless boats all the way from Peterhof: "Imagine this park all lit up. In this freezing country deprived of daylight, the illuminations were like a forest fire: it might be said that the night became a consolation for the passing day. The trees disappeared beneath a decoration of diamonds; in each lane there were as many Chinese lanterns as leaves: it was Asia, not the real Asia, or modern Asia, but the storybook Baghdad of *A Thousand and One Nights*, or the most mystical Babylon of Semiramis." Time permitting, vessels of the imperial navy came up to the shore and fired salvos in honor of the empress. During Custine's stay, a storm prevented guests from enjoying this added spectacle. But worse, some boats coming from the capital capsized in the gulf, drowning hundreds of people. No one ever knew it, and no one mentioned the disastrous event, because it would mean, "upsetting the Empress and accusing the Emperor."

Pampered by the imperial couple, Custine was admitted into the intimate family circle at Alexandria. It was a distinguished honor, since invitations came from the tsarina alone. During the empress's birthday celebration, Custine was again privileged to stay in two dressing rooms that belonged to actors of the Court Theater. His lodgings were not far from the Grand Palace, where nothing was lacking except a bed.

22   Fortunately, Custine never went anywhere without his little iron cot, "an indispensable object for a European traveling in Russia." Many courtiers had to camp in more precarious conditions. Charmed by the fragile grace of the empress, he was impressed by "the noble figure of Nicholas, whose head dominated all the others."

At the same time as the cottage, Nicholas had a little church built at Alexandria. Shaped like a medieval shrine, it was dedicated to Saint Alexander Nevsky. As early as 1829, Nicholas left its creation up to Karl Friedrich Schinkel (1781–1841). At this time, the architect was converting the little castle of Charlottenhof in the Sans-Souci Park near Berlin for Friedrich Wilhelm II, the tsarina's father, while he was waiting to restore the ruins of Stolzenfels for the Prince of Prussia, the latter's brother. The choice of this famous architect, closely allied to the Prussian court, could only have been attractive to Alexandra Feodorovna. Several years later, in 1838, she commissioned her brother, the crown prince, to create the design for a summer palace at Orianda, on the rocky coast of Crimea. The tsarina wanted "something like Siam." This was the often-used family name that was given to Charlottenhof Palace, because the distant land of Siam was considered an Eden or symbol of liberty. But the project puffed up like the frog in the fable.[15] At first conceived in the Gothic style, it emerged as a colossal acropolis, "the largest imperial palace on earth," according to Schinkel. To this grandiose dream, White Rose would have preferred a simpler little house.

LEFT: Architect Andrei Stacken-schneider designed the paneled dining room in 1842. The table is full of the porcelain and crystal banquet service decorated with the royal coat of arms designed by the poet Vasili Joukovski for the Alexandria estate (overleaf). Made in the Imperial Factories of St. Petersburg (1827–1829), 5,210 pieces of this service were produced during the nineteenth century.

OPPOSITE: A marble reproduction of "The Wrestlers," made after the famous ancient original, which is now in the Uffizi Gallery in Florence.

In the cottage library, works of Romantic writers and poets stand alongside the legislative code of the Russian empire, published during Nicholas's reign.

OPPOSITE: In front of the window, is a model of the little castle on Peacock Island. This was a residence for Kings Friedrich Wilhelm II and Friedrich Wilhelm III of Prussia.

BELOW: The folding screen in painted leather engraved and gilded is also German.

LEFT: Detail of one of the sculpted oak armchairs in the library.

OVERLEAF: In the tsarina's parlor, on the marble mantle sculpted by Trisconi in 1828, is a clock inspired by Rouen Cathedral's south portal, according to the inscription on a plate affixed to its base. It is flanked by two candelabras and two Sèvres vases, which were presented to Tsar Alexander I by Napoleon I.

Cathedrale de Rouen
portail du midi

OPPOSITE: In the small study: family memorabilia surrounded the tsarina. Above the bust of her youngest daughter, made by Ivan Vitali and dating from 1847, is the portrait of her eldest daughter Olga Nikolaievna in medieval dress. It is the work of Timoléon von Neft, a court painter.

BELOW: A bronze miniature of the funeral monument of Queen Louise of Prussia, mother of the tsarina, made by Christian Daniel Rauch.

RIGHT: A mahogany sideboard adorned with a mirror dating from the 1830s.

OVERLEAF: This bust of Alexandra Feodorovna by Rauch (left) decorates the tsar's study. The silversmith Georg Hossauer made the silver rose (right) given to the tsarina during a grandiose ceremony called "The Miracle of the White Rose" and held in honor of her birthday on June 13, 1829 at Potsdam Castle. "White Rose" was the empress's nickname.

H O H E N S C H W A N G A U

HOHENSCHWANGAU CASTLE

Prince Maximilian Joseph;

later King Maximilian II of Bavaria

Queen Marie of Bavaria; née Princess of Hohenzollern

King Louis or Ludwig II of Bavaria

On June 9, 1886, the little Bavarian castle of Hohenschwangau witnessed a gloomy reception. On that day, after lunching in Munich with Prince Leopold, uncle of King Ludwig II and the future regent of Bavaria, a special committee of statesmen and doctors sat in a parlor car aboard a train bound for Oberstdorf. At the station, the harnessed horses and carriages waited. Their destination was Hohenschwangau. At the castle, "The Supper of His Majesty the King" consisted of no fewer than seven courses, according to the menu. Champagne and beer flowed copiously in the dining room where members of the committee had gathered. On Bismarck's advice, Prince Leopold warned the German princes and the emperor of Austria about certain facts concerning his "beloved and illustrious nephew." The prince is "inaccessible to the princes of his royal house and advisors of the Crown, unapproachable even to his secretaries and the aides employed in his personal service. Invisible to his people, the sovereign has relationships only with those of the most humble station or those on whom depend the most important issues of concern to the court and the State." Moreover, "his inordinate spending for extremely costly building projects has provoked a very grave crisis for the coffers of the Cabinet."

From this moment on, the process leading to deposing the king became inevitable. After dinner, members of the committee put on their uniforms. Some wore Hussar's jackets, some dressed in black outfits, and all were studded with decorations. In the middle of the night they proceeded to the nearby Neuschwanstein Castle, where Ludwig II lived. The curtain opened on the final act of Ludwig II's life.

Hohenschwangau was a cozy nest where the ruler called the "Mad King" spent his childhood and adolescence. It was a little yellow diamond hewn into facets with very simple symmetry, and set between two lakes, in the immense jewel box of mountains covered with pine trees that were almost black in color. In an earlier time, Hohenschwangau Castle reigned alone over the formidable countryside, until the construction of Neuschwanstein, which, from that time on, would seem to look down scornfully on it from the height of its inaccessible rock.

Built in the twelfth century, the castle was the residence of the lords from Schwangau, the "Land of the Swan." Hohenschwangau witnessed the birth of one of the great Germanic myths, amplified in the Romantic age. According to legend, Lohengrin, a knight of the Holy Grail, appeared here on a skiff harnessed to a swan. A monumental swan of stone looks down over the roofs of the present castle, lacing its long neck down the pole from which the royal standard is hoisted. The castle is also linked to the history of the Bavarian royal family, since a Wittelsbach, Duke Albert V, Dürer's patron, lived here in the sixteenth century.

In 1832 the *Kronprinz* (Crown Prince) Maximilian bought the land of Schwangau and decided to direct attention to the old fortified castle, which at that time lay mostly in ruins. Restoration began in 1833. Three years later, the castle was habitable. Paradoxically, the old fort devastated by the Napoleonic wars was reconstructed by Maximilian, heir to the royal crown offered by the emperor to his grandfather, Max-Joseph, first duke then king of Bavaria under the name Maximilian I.

40

The taste of the time was toward neither archaeologically accurate restorations nor pedantic evocations. Instead it was through the novels of Sir Walter Scott, the dramas of Schiller, and the stories and legends collected by the Brothers Grimm that a Romantic vision of the Middle Ages was formulated. At Hohenschwangau a mixture of literary musing and the comfortable Biedermeier style boasting blond woods and mahogany evoked the Middle Ages. The crown prince did not choose a seasoned, experienced architect to be in charge, but his former drawing teacher, the talented Dominik or rather Domenico Quaglio (Munich 1787– Hohenschwangau 1837). Born into a family of theater decorators, he spent sixteen years creating scenery for the court theatre in Munich. The workers soon nicknamed him "the Tyrant of the Castle."

Maximilian's decision spoke for itself. Rather than seeking out the best German architects, he chose dream and illusion over the materiality of architectural form. After Quaglio's death, architect Joseph Daniel Ohlmüller, designer of the *Mariahilfkirche* (Church of Our Lady of Good Hope, 1831–1839) in Munich, was commissioned to build on the site. He added a new tower in 1838 and raised the height of some of the existing towers. With the marriage of Maximilian in 1842, and then with his ascension to the throne in 1848, came more enlargements such as the lodging for princes and knights. Another architect from Munich, Georg Friedrich Ziebland, who had built the imposing Saint Boniface Basilica for Ludwig I, successfully completed these final projects.

Maximilian did not have the flair of his father, Ludwig I. Ludwig had made Munich into "a New Athens" before having to renounce his throne, following his scandalous liaison that proved ruinous for the state, with the dancer Lola Montès. Inspired by the writings of Emperor Marcus Aurelius, Maximilian instead dreamed of putting philosophy on the throne of Bavaria. Dull and boring, he married Marie of Hohenzollern (1825–1889), princess of Prussia and sister of the future emperor of Germany, Wilhelm I. Athletic and angelically beautiful, she helped encourage the sport of mountain climbing and also bragged about never having had the patience to read a single book.

Hohenschwangau owes its distinctiveness less to its symmetrical, simply decorated facades and more to its rich interior decorations. The painted murals that adorn each room are by the famous Viennese painter, Moritz von Schwind (1804–1871), whose watercolors have been preserved. In *Le voyage romantique, Chez Louis II de Bavière*, published in 1910, Ferdinand Bac mentions this Romantic artist. "From 1820 to 1870, [von Schwind], better than any other, brought his stories to German speaking people as something of a resurgence of ancient stories from a long ago past." These stories thus arrived onto the painter's palette from the depths of the Middle Ages, which did not know the gilt-edged books given as gifts at New Year's time.[16] And he evoked them with naive, sensual charm and an intense flavor." The walls came alive with numerous scenes taken from great national legends such as the *Nibelungenlied*, Tristan and Isolde, King Pepin and *Berthe au Grand Pied*.[17]

LEFT: *Prince Maximilian Feeding the Swans*, by Lorenzo Quaglio, 1821.

RIGHT: The garden of the castle and the lion's fountain, watercolor by Wilhelm Scheuchzer, ca. 1860. The fountain was constructed according to Domenico Quaglio's design.

BELOW: Maximilian II, Queen Marie, the Princes Ludwig (on the right) and Othon in the park at Hohenschwangau, lithograph of J. Woelffle according to a design by Erich Coriens.

ABOVE: Crown Prince Ludwig at the age of five, a lithograph made from a watercolor by Ernst Rietschl, in 1850. At this young age, he was already interested in architecture.

To the future King Ludwig II, painters were the equivalent of a magic lantern, just as in the case of another very sensitive child, the narrator in Marcel Proust's *Remembrance of Things Past*. He was captivated by the adventures of Genevieve de Brabant and Golo the Knight "full of fearful intent" as they marched along the walls of his bedroom.[18]

In the interior of the castle, swans reign without peer throughout the decor. Twelve swans crowned with candles decorate the large chandelier in Queen Marie's reception room. Swans with wings spread out are ensconced on the tops of stately centerpieces done in silver and vermeil, presented by the city of Augsburg as a wedding gift to Maximilian. Still other swans are curled up against numerous porcelain vases that the future Ludwig II's mother collected. And not-to-be forgotten, flesh-and-blood birds slide along the lake below the castle. King in his turn, how could Ludwig not have succumbed to the universe of Richard Wagner's operas, when he, as a child, had been nourished on the legend of the swan? And would it not continue, until one day he would die from it, drowned in Starnberg Lake, another "Swan Lake"?

When Maximilian died in 1864, the queen mother held court at Hohenschwangau, which Ludwig regretfully agreed to share with her. He wrote to Wagner on August 27, 1867, "My beloved Hohenschwangau which, when I am alone here, is for me a great source of solitude, peace, and true poetry, changes before my eyes [when there with his mother] into a sorrowful retreat."

LEFT: The castle with the Hall of Heroes and Knights.

RIGHT: A portrait of Ludwig II of Bavaria that is now kept in the Room of Reigning Princes at Miramare Castle.

Hohenschwangau was the only residence of Ludwig II where Richard Wagner, whom he called "My Wotan," ever stayed. The musician wrote to the king on November 11, 1865, the day of his arrival at Hohenschwangau: "Here I am in the *burg* of the Grail, under the sublime protection of Perceval's love. The sun is laughing at this unreal reality. I am happy, happy to the very fiber of my being."

When Wagner died in Venice in 1883, it was at Hohenschwangau that Ludwig II mourned his very dearest friend. Draped in black crepe, the blond maple piano on which the composer played for him alone would forever remain mute. From that time on, Hohenschwangau would be a privileged witness to Ludwig's inescapable flight from the affairs of the throne, from life in general, and from Munich in particular. Munich was the hated city, about which the king had said: "Six white elephants cannot make me return there."

It was from Hohenschwangau that some of his crazy nocturnal escapades started. Ferdinand Bac recorded this story by one of the king's former groomsmen: "His Majesty had a habit of waking me at all hours of the day and night. He would call me to his bed and say: 'Nicodemus, it's a lovely night tonight, we leave in an hour. Get the blue and silver harnesses.' Then, he would tell me which horses. The King would arrive wrapped in a big white coat. Often, horsemen would ride before and follow the carriage with resin torches." Taking off at breakneck speed, the horses would run, mouths foaming, into difficult passes on dangerous slopes cut into ravines by rain or else covered with icy snow. Then, suddenly, they would all have to stop to enjoy the moonlight. Sometimes the king would spend an entire night going around a lake where he would take pleasure in following the golden reflections that the electric lights from his carriage cast.

To the eyes of today's visitor, Hohenschwangau remains the castle where the prince was an eternal child, a prisoner of chivalric dreams that emerged from rooms covered in paintings, and from the blue bedroom where the sky was strewn with stars. Hohenschwangau is the house of childhood, matrix of the dreams that forged the imagination of one of the most enigmatic personages in history.

Ludwig II and his cousin, Sophia of Wittelsbach, in a photograph by Jozef Albert, 1867. Following the scandal caused by his friendship with Wagner, the engagement in 1867 of the king to his cousin Sophia, sister of Empress Elizabeth, seemed promising. He called her Elsa; he would be her Lohengrin. But before the end of the year, he broke off the engagement and wrote in his diary: "Finally, I am coming out of this terrible nightmare." Sophia became the Duchess of Alençon, and perished in 1897 in a fire at the Bazar de la Charité in Paris.[19]

OPPOSITE: From the window of his bedroom, Ludwig II could look out with a telescope on the progress of Neuschwanstein Castle's construction.

46

OTTO DER ERLAUCHTE
PFALZGRAF BEY RHEIN HERZOG IN BAYERN.

LEFT: Othon the Magnificent, one of the heroes depicted in a series of bronzes, by Ludwig von Schwanthaler (1837–1842) that adorn the Schyrenzimmer, the Room of the Counts of Pfaltz-Scheyen, distant ancestors of Maximilian.

OPPOSITE: The paintings in the Oriental room recall a trip to Italy, Greece, and Asia Minor that Maximilian took in 1833 when he was still just the crown prince of Bavaria. Under the yoke of the Ottoman Empire, a stricken Greece awakened enormous sympathy in Europe during the Romantic era, and especially the sympathy of Ludwig I of Bavaria, Maximilian's father. The House of Bavaria gave Greece her first king, Othon I, brother of Maximilian, who raised Athens from its ruins. The Oriental room served as a bedroom for Queen Marie who became a widow in 1854. She gladly held court at Hohenschwangau.

PAGES 44–45: As a mythic place where Lohengrin appeared on a skiff driven by a swan, Hohenschwangau—restored and decorated by Maximilian of Bavaria—devoted part of its decor to this hero. The passion of the future Ludwig II for German legends and later for the operas of Wagner was born in this dining room where, as a child, he had numerous meals facing the paintings designed by Moritz von Schwind. Surmounted by crowned swans, the imposing silver and vermeil centerpiece was a wedding gift from the town of Augsburg to King Maximilian and Queen Marie, grand-daughter of the king of Prussia, Friedrich Wilhelm II. At Hohenschwangau, the queen collected numerous porcelains recalling the legend of the swan.

OVERLEAF: In the Hall of Entertainments, mural paintings recount the epic of Theodoric the Great, king of the Ostrogoths. The stately centerpiece on the neoclassical table came from the *Residenz* in Munich.

50

LEFT: A marble bust of Richard Wagner evokes the passionate friendship that Ludwig II accorded him throughout his life. During his stay at Hohenschwangau in November 1865, the composer would awaken his patron with the sounds of the music of Lohengrin. Shortly after this date there was a fireworks display on the Alpsee and a "perfectly recreated" performance of Lohengrin's arrival in his skiff drawn by a swan. On the day of his departure, Ludwig II gave the composer a watch painted with the image of the knight with a swan, the legend that was a source for his "enthusiasm" and his "burning love" for the composer.

OPPOSITE: Connecting with the Hohenstaufen room, a small chapel was planned in 1840 in one of the towers where Maximilian's library had been. Tsar Alexander II presented the two icons that decorate the altar to Ludwig II. The bas-relief representing Christ is the work of the Danish artist Bertel Thorwaldsen.

OVERLEAF: Bathed in bluish light, the mural paintings in the Tasso bedroom (left) recount the love of Armida and Rinaldo.[20] This bedroom belonged to Maximilian before Ludwig II. Oil lamps made the crystal stars inlaid in the ceiling light up.

Richard Wagner, as a guest of Ludwig II, slept in this bedroom decorated with paintings representing the love of Authari and Theodelinde[21]. Painted according to the neoclassic canon, these scenes possess the crisp sharpness of medieval illuminations.

In Maximilian's study, the sculpted cedar furniture recalls a repertory of arcs, ceiling roses, and curly rosettes borrowed from Gothic architecture. Contemporaneous to the novels of Walter Scott and the dramas of Schiller, these creations were not concerned with archaeological exactitude. The small statue below is of Friedrich II (the Wise), prince elector of Saxony, who died in 1556. It belongs to the series of bronzes executed between 1837 and 1842 by Ludwig von Schwanthaler.

OVERLEAF LEFT: Framed in gilt foliage, this painting depicts the return of a knight after a Crusade.

OVERLEAF RIGHT: Placed near a neo-Gothic clock, a gilded bronze represents Frederick the Conqueror, prince elector of Saxony who died in 1476 (right).

The Room of the Feudal Ladies took a particularly long time to lay out. Maximilian wanted the decorations to illustrate the "ideal life" of feudal ladies in the Middle Ages, and he took great pains to consult experts. It is probable that different artists did the mural paintings but only one, *The Harp Player* by Friedrich Giessman, has been signed.

OPPOSITE: The small statue on the dresser is a bronze by Ferdinand von Miller (1879). It represents the Regent Prince Leopold, the uncle and successor of Ludwig II.

LEFT: On the fireplace opposite, two plaster casts by Johann Halbig (1855) are displayed. They portray Princes Ludwig and Othon at the ages of six and three.

ABOVE: A typically Bavarian earthenware stove, made from refractory stone.

STOLZENFELS

Traveling in 1815 on the banks of the Rhine, Crown Prince Friedrich Wilhelm wrote, "Standing before thousands of divine castles and craggy rocks and mountains and torrents, I have been overcome with bliss." Some twenty years afterward, Victor Hugo followed the same course of this vast river. There he saw "in the transparency of its waves, the past as well as the future of Europe." He watched the magnificent steamships decked with flags, sailboats loaded with bundles, large boats pulled by a good little horse, much like "an ant pulls a dead scarab." He saw the medieval fortresses crowning the mountains, the valleys filled with fog, the wooden trains boldly crossing the torrents and waterfalls of the river. Near the city of Koblenz, he raised his eyes toward "the magnificent ruins" of Stolzenfels Castle, situated not far from the mythic *Konigstuhl* (Seat of Kings) where the archbishop electors and palatine counts used to choose their kings in the fourteenth century. Hugo did not know that the prince of Prussia planned to make Stolzenfels his favorite residence in the Rhineland.

Built on the left bank of the Rhine, and perched on a rock that prevented attack on three sides because of its steep slopes, the castle is protected on the fourth side by a gorge that cuts deeply into the rock. Stolzenfels Castle—literally, the Proud Rock—overlooks the river for about four hundred feet, at the point where it joins the Lahn. At its feet sits the ancient village of Kapellen, founded by the Romans. From the towers of Stolzenfels, the view tumbles down to the immense Rhineland plain and follows the beautiful ribbon of the Rhine to Koblenz, called Confluentia by the Romans, up to where the Moselle meets its monarch.

The seat of the Department of the Rhine-and-Moselle in 1798, this city was given to Prussia in 1815. In 1823 the city presented the incredible ruins of Stolzenfels to the royal prince of Prussia, the future Friedrich Wilhelm IV. When night fell on September 14, 1842, a strange procession of torch-carriers, knights on horseback, and damsels brightly gleaming in their rainbow-colored costumes from ancient times, climbed up the rock in the direction of the castle. King Friedrich Wilhelm and his family were taking possession of the ancient residence, and the castle was celebrating the six hundredth anniversary of its founding.

Erected between 1242 and 1259 by Arnold von Isenburg, archbishop of Trier, who at the time sought to protect Koblenz with newly built fortifications, Stolzenfels was at the heart of one of the great principalities of the ancient Germanic empire. The fourteenth century saw the perfection of Stolzenfels. At that time Archbishop Werner probably built the large residence facing the river. Additions or repairs to the ancient structure would continue until the seventeenth century. During the Thirty Years War, the castle was taken several times by the Swedes and the French. Louis XIV's army finally burned it in 1688, during the unsuccessful siege on Koblenz. In the eighteenth century, what had been the proud residence of the archbishops of Trier was valued only at the cost of its building material, and reduced to the negligible glory of a pile of rocks.

As soon as he was in possession of Stolzenfels, a place that spoke so well to his unbridled imagination, Friedrich Wilhelm expressed a desire to make it his residence.

63

64

The decision to integrate the Rhineland into the kingdom of Prussia was certainly not foreign to the political wishes of the Hohenzollerns. Yet it also showed the sincere enthusiasm of the most romantic of the Prussian princes, whose only true passion was architecture. He commissioned the architect Johann Claudius von Lassaulx, inspector of the district of Koblenz, to survey and submit a design for reconstruction. Lassaulx suggested a restoration of the main dwelling, a rectangular tower consisting of three floors that was better preserved than the rest of the building. While respecting the integrity of this medieval structure, he proposed enriching it with windows in various forms, encircling it with sculptured friezes, and decorating it with wrought iron bars. In Berlin, the prince showed these plans to his favorite, if not his master-architect, Karl Friedrich Schinkel, and invited him to submit his own design. Literally obsessed by architecture, the prince placed limitless confidence in Schinkel, who often would give form to the prince's own ideas. The premature death of Schinkel in 1841, soon after the ascension to the throne of Friedrich Wilhelm, deprived the monarch of a much-needed advisor.

At Stolzenfels, more respectful than his predecessor of the original appearance of the building and the rhythm of its unadorned masses—so much so that he decided to take off the roofs—Schinkel arrived at an impressive and majestic composition. His plans were not limited to the residence but also included the eastern wing of the castle. But in 1824, only the access road to Stolzenfels had been built. In the meantime, a new work site was opened by the restoration of another Rhineland castle, Rheinstein, toward which all the energy and important sums of money were directed. Prussia played a role in underscoring a mythic Germanic past, the creation of which would help to forge German unity. While waiting, Schinkel transformed the old apartments of Friedrich II at the royal castle of Berlin.

Would Stolzenfels emerge one day from its ruins? Its destiny remained uncertain. In 1834, a picturesque garden around its old outer walls was envisioned. Finally in 1835, reconstruction began. But the architectural elevations and designs of Lasssaulx had been lost. Schinkel therefore proceeded anew with a survey of the existing ruins. The following year, the crown prince approved his design. At the suggestion of von Wussow, commander of the Ehrenbreitstein Fortress, a soldier, Captain Naumann, was made responsible for executing the plans. In Prussia, where military order reigned supreme, architecture also stood at attention. There, supreme elegance merged with an almost spartan rigor.

The main residence and postern were completed in 1837. The architect then proceeded methodically to reconstruct the other apartments. A notable change was brought to the 1836 design: a vaulted cellar was transformed into a summer room, opening to the future pergola and the main courtyard. This elegant structure, held up by thin columns, recalls one of Schinkel's most beautiful Gothic designs, Queen Louise's mausoleum. It was never built, but the explanatory notice is a veritable manifesto in favor of Gothic architecture, undeniably superior (according to its author) to classical antiquity, to which it was nonetheless an accomplice.

ABOVE: Two views of the main courtyard attached to the garden of the
pergola by an elegant vaulted
passageway. The same garden (right)
painted in a watercolor by Caspar
Scheuren in 1845. The two people
dressed in the style of the fifteenth century are reminiscent of the costumed
ball held to dedicate Stolzenfels. In
olden times reserved for the eminent of
this world, peacocks confirm the
princely rank of this residence.

However, Schinkel preferred to redo the central tower in
the same yellow ochre as the other buildings, rather than
painting it red as it originally had been.

As in the Middle Ages, protecting the entrance to the
castle, the majestic chapel exists today, designed by the
engineer Karl Schnitzler. The Cologne Cathedral, which
Friedrich Wilhelm worked on, inspired this elegant Gothic
structure striated with fine ribbing.

At the death of Schinkel in 1841, the design of Stolzenfels grew in scope once more. This time a west wing was
added, parallel to the east wing that looked out over the
Rhine, and that replaced the wall that was initially
designed. This new project gave the overall design a symmetry that was quite foreign to the original castle constructed by the archbishop of Trier. The lower courtyard
to the north was transformed, linking the central portion
of the castle to the Adjutant's Tower, into a pergola. A
watercolor by Caspar Scheuren dating from 1845
(above), recalls this structure at the time of its splendor;
a vine winds around its columns, rendered even more
slender by the artist's brush. Peacocks gambol on the
ground that is covered with geometric paving stones in
alternating colors, beneath the gaze of two people in
puffed out knee breeches in fifteenth-century style. Now
eaten away by moisture, this wooden pergola is a
poignant sight. Crossing it, one passes across centuries.
The dream of a comfortable Middle Ages, born in the full-
ness of the nineteenth century, seems so far away from
our own preoccupations that it becomes "medievalized"
before our very eyes.

A marble statue of Friedrich Wilhelm IV decorates the summer room (below) tiled in blue and white. On sunny days, this huge airy room, with its ribbed vaults (above), served as a dining area for the royal family.

Here a fanciful imitation, with no archaeological foundation, incites the same emotion as the original. To add to the confusion, the visitor notices an authentic stone fireplace sculpted in the sixteenth century, taken from a house in Cologne (page 68) and placed in the passageway leading to the summer room. At Stolzenfels, the back and forth between the ancient and the modern are constant. Vestiges of the medieval castle are encompassed in nineteenth century construction, but those who are able to distinguish one from the other are very clever indeed.

Preserving its essential decor and original furnishings, Stolzenfels attests to the elegant surroundings in which Friedrich Wilhelm and his wife, Elizabeth of Wittelsbach, princess of Bavaria, lived. There was no place here for the strict etiquette of the Berlin palace or the official residence in Koblenz, where the royals held court. The Gothic dream was originally decorated with precious paintings, today replaced with copies. Some antique furniture, like the pulpit of Johann Hugo Van Orsbeck, archbishop elector of Trier, made in Antwerp around 1700, seems to bless the historical recreations of the 1840s.

When Schinkel died, King Friedrich Wilhelm lost an invaluable mentor. He became a reactionary, and the former liberal refused the imperial crown that the National Assembly of Frankfurt offered him in 1849. Diagnosed with dementia in 1858, he left the throne to his brother Wilhelm, the regent and future emperor of Germany.

OPPOSITE: Supported by two slender columns of black marble, the vault of the Great Hall of Knights takes some liberties with its thirteenth-century models. The military trophies and weapons hanging on the wall, nonetheless, attempt to evoke the authentic Middle Ages.

After 1841, the north courtyard was changed into an interior garden and equipped with a pergola in painted wood. The pergola, in an illusionary manner, carries out some authentic medieval vestiges. The walls that enclose it date from the fourteenth century. However faded today, the colors imitate the gray of stone and are faithful to Friedrich Wilhelm's time.

BELOW: In the vaulted passage leading to the Adjutant's Tower is a sculpted stone fireplace from the sixteenth century, taken from a house in Cologne.
At Stolzenfels, the nineteenth century informally mixes with surviving medieval remnants creating the illusion of a bygone era. These are "the remembrance of things past."[22]

In spite of its pretension as a "little hall" of knights, this vaulted room in blue and gold is equipped with comfortable mid-nineteenth century padded furniture. Tile parquet and high-paneling of sculpted wood reinforce its inviting character, which adapted well to its primary function as a parlor for the future prince of Prussia, Friedrich Wilhelm IV. Fresco scenes illustrating knightly virtues decorate the walls with episodes from the lives of Geoffroi de Bouillon, Frederick Barbarossa, John of Bohemia, Philippe de' Souabe, and Rudolph von Habsburg. Hermann Stilke, their creator, was a student of the great Peter Cornelius, director of the Academy of Munich beginning in 1825. The emperor Friedrich Wilhelm called him to Berlin in 1840.

OVERLEAF: A detail of a chair in the queen's parlor (left). Conceived in a more bourgeois style, the queen's reception room (right) exchanges vaulted ribbing for a striated wooded ceiling and fresco for floral-inspired damask. In fact, official receptions took place at the Koblenz castles and not at Stolzenfels, where court etiquette was less strict. The seats, while respecting Gothic inspiration, have the curves of the comfortable furniture of the time.

71

PAGES 74–75: The curtains in the queen's parlor were cut from brocade from Lyon, and were recently remade according to the originals. The same fabric with Moorish motifs covers the seats. This corner room has an exceptional view of the Rhine River where it meets the Lahn, and has one of the most pleasant views in the castle. A polyptych painted by Peter Cornelius has been placed above the writing table.

OPPOSITE: Leading into the queen's parlor, this entirely paneled boudoir was set up in one of the towers of the castle. Inspired by Renaissance art, the sumptuously sculpted double desk (right and below) is the work of an artist from Neuweid named Johann Wilhelm Vetter. It bears the date 1842.

OVERLEAF: With a refinement reminiscent of British castles, the dressing room of the king (left) and that of the queen (right) are wainscotted halfway up in oak. Invited to Stolzenfels, in the company of Prince Albert three years after the dedication of the castle in 1842, Queen Victoria so liked being there, it is said, that she missed the performances at the Koblenz Opera.

Adorned by a little corner fireplace with a hearth tiled in blue
and white, the king's bedroom
(opposite and below) is of rustic
simplicity. The antechamber
(right) contains an unusual
sculpted cabinet flanked by
twisted columns. It is, in fact, a
fragment of a piece of furniture
from the seventeenth century,
completed in the nineteenth century with tiers of drawers.

PAGES 80–81: In a sleeping room
destined for the royal couple, the
seats with simple moldings are
upholstered in green and fitted
with copper pulls to make them
easier to move around (left). Comfort also reigned in the king's
room (right), where the furniture is
draped in red velvet and fringed.

Finished in 1845, the immense chapel is decorated with paintings on gold backgrounds, done by Ernst Deger, an artist from Remagen, a little town in the Rhine region. The paintings depict the story of Adam and Eve, the sacrifice of Isaac, and scenes from the life of Christ (pages 85–89). Attributed to Karl Schnitzler, this elegant structure was partly inspired by the Cologne cathedral, restored at the bidding of Friedrich Wilhelm by the architect Ernst Friedrich Zwirner around 1842. He also restored the Gothic Remagen Church. Besides its remarkable original sculpted wood furniture and cast iron staircase that leads to the gallery, the chapel has preserved all its painted, stenciled decoration and gold inlay, filtered by an unreal light that the stained-glass grisaille allows in.

PENA

PENA PALACE

Prince Ferdinand Auguste of Saxe-Coburg-Gotha;
later King Fernando II of Portugal

Queen Maria II of Portugal; née Princess of Braganza

September 1834: an auction was organized to sell the contents of the monastery of Pena, in Sintra, an area near Lisbon. It was a result of the new Portuguese law dissolving religious orders. At this time, "the enclosure and buildings of said monastery" were offered for rent. When no offer was made, the monastery was put up for sale, but with the stipulation that the buyer must guarantee its preservation. It was a "national monument, and the church boasted a finely sculpted altarpiece." On November 3, 1838, Ferdinand Auguste of Saxe-Coburg-Gotha, future king of Portugal, found himself the buyer of it all.

Looming up from the north of Lisbon, the tumultuous Serra de Sintra spills into the ocean at Cabo de Roca. From this extraordinary mass of lacy rock, invaded by seaweed, ferns, and green oaks, their thirst quenched by numerous sources, many mythic stories sprang forth. Geographers of antiquity identified it as the Sacred Mountain—Ptolemy called it "Mountain of the Moon"—and it conceals megaliths that attest a devotion to it since prehistoric times. In the tenth century, the geographer Al-Bacri praised the city of Sintra, perched on the northern slope of the Serra, for its healthy climate, the longevity of its inhabitants, and the extraordinary size of its fruit. Lord Byron who, in *Childe Harold* sings of this "glorious Eden," confirmed a common opinion in the nineteenth century. The royal court of Portugal did not wait for the lyrical effusions of a poet to establish its residence at the site of a thirteenth-century fortress.

It is necessary to travel several miles and climb a hill to reach the *Castelo da Pena*. One passes alongside the house where Byron found the inspiration for his poem. Continuing the ascent, one discovers the ruins of the Moorish castle with crenellated walls. Finally, at a height of about 1,640 feet, the gate leading to Pena Castle appears. One must still pass through a Moorish gate, take one's chances crossing a drawbridge, and traverse a vaulted gallery to reach the castle. With its artificial turrets, edges beveled like pieces of a chessboard, and its imbroglio of minarets and cupolas, the castle compares to none other. What its freshly white-washed facades, in lively colors of pale yellow, red, blue gray, and salmon hide, is that far from being born all at once, such a singular architectural curiosity embraces building from several eras.

Ancient stories tell of a miraculous apparition of the Virgin on Pena Rock. This miracle has attracted the faithful since the twelfth century. King Manuel I created an access to this steep location, and then founded a monastery, a modest wooden building, to commemorate the voyage of Vasco da Gama to the Indies. According to legend, the monarch would view, from this promontory, the return of his flotilla as it approached the mouth of the Tagus River. The king later presented the monastery of *Nossa Sehnora da Pena* (Our Lady of Pena) to the Order of Hieronymites. Around 1511, the monastery was rebuilt in more lasting and solid stone. The great earthquake of 1755 that devastated Lisbon and the surrounding area dealt a severe blow to the structure.

In 1838, when Dom Fernando became the owner, the ancient monastery of Pena was composed of a vaulted cloister onto which twelve cells opened.

The design of the new postern (top) is attributed to Dom Fernando II himself, around 1843; below is a detail of the first postern decorated with the royal coat of arms and seal.

ABOVE: The French sculptor Nicolas Chaterenne created the chapel altarpiece (see details, pages 106–107).

RIGHT: The palace during its construction (photographed ca. 1880).

OPPOSITE: The Triton Arc supports the bow window of the Indian room.

PAGES 90–91: The castle dominates rocks in strange shapes, once known as the Holy Mountain. Powerful buttresses crowned by false crenellated turrets protect the access slope to the chapel (page 93).

MEDALLION (PAGE 92): Queen Doña Amelia and her son Dom Manuel II were photographed on the castle's terrace.

The chapel, the sacristy and the tower are situated at an oblique angle from the cloister. This asymmetric design endows the restored building with a picturesque quality while adding to it.

Ferdinand Auguste of Saxe-Coburg-Gotha landed in Lisbon on April 8, 1836, at the age of nineteen, after a journey aboard the war vessel *Manchester*. From his childhood at Rosenau Castle near Coburg in the center of Germany, as part of an illustrious family allied to all the reigning houses in Europe, Ferdinand had acquired a refined, artistic background, supported by the wealth of his mother, whose maiden name was Princess Kohary. A designer of note, in Vienna he expressed his artistic bent playing Schubert and Franz Liszt's music. Later he would take great joy in welcoming the latter to Lisbon.

His future bride Doña Maria II da Gloria (1819–1853) incarnated the liberal and constitutional cause in Portugal and was proclaimed queen at age fifteen after the tragic days of the civil war. This daughter of Dom Pedro I of Brazil (Dom Pedro IV of Portugal) and Archduchess Leopoldine of Austria, was born in Rio de Janeiro. The widow of Auguste Charles de Beauharnais, Duke of Leuchetenberg, she then married Ferdinand of Saxe-Coburg-Gotha by proxy on January 1, 1836. She was to give him ten children but died in childbirth with the eleventh. At the birth of the heir to the throne in 1837, the future Pedro V, the prince consort became king and commander-in-chief of the army under the name Fernando II.

Preferring the language of arts to that of arms, Fernando quickly put an end to a humiliatingly mediocre military career. The Marquesa de Fronteira recounts how one day, the king was crossing the Tagus to review some troops stationed on the other side. They lost track of him, only to learn that he was in the house of a navy accountant, singing a duet from Handel's *Semiramis* with the young daughter of the house. *O rei artista*, the artist king, easily wielded the paint brush, chisel, and scalpel for sculpting in clay. A collector of paintings, majolica, and porcelain, he frequently visited the Sacavem ceramics manufacture. His taste for medieval architecture led to his interest in major monuments in Portugal such as the monastery of the Hieronymites at Belèm, the Batalha Monastery, for which he developed a sort of passion and the famous *Convento de Cristo* in Tomar. An intense curiosity for the remnants of Portugal's renowned past found its expression in the process of restoring and improving Pea. With the exception of certain textbook like copies, such as the sacristy window of the *Convento de Cristo*, this historical knowledge did not lead to cold imitations but rather to works full of originality, where great examples from the past were interpreted with unbridled whimsy.

Conceived and perhaps designed by the king himself, Castle Pena's postern borrowed its watchtowers from Belèm. But its stones, cut to diamond points, recall those of the famous *Casa dos Bicos* in Lisbon. The doorframe with its cannonballs was copied from *Cunhal das Bolas*, in Barrio Alto, yet this meringuelike covering evokes a Mughal India. Mixed in this composition is a collection of mysterious symbolic emblems such as two intertwined serpents, or the wolf corpses that surmount the Cross of the Order of Christ.

To renovate Pena, Dom Fernando passed over Possidonio da Silva, architect of the royal palaces, giving wide range to his compatriot, Baron Wilhelm von Eschwege. A native of the Rhineland, this enigmatic personality fought in the Portuguese army against the French in 1807. Afterwards he displayed the talents, one after another, of a naturalist, geologist, director of mines in Brazil, and military engineer. His interest in architecture can no doubt be explained by the desire of a financial backer to keep a close eye on the work he commissioned, much in the same way as King Carol I did for his castle in the Carpathian Mountains.[23] The primary architect of Pena was thus the monarch himself. In addition, Eschwege was a cultured man, who knew well the works of Goethe and Humboldt, and who, it is thought, read Schinkel's essay on the excellence of the Gothic style and its connection to nature. It is certain that he was familiar with Stolzenfels and Babelsberg castles, the former built by Schinkel for Friedrich Wilhelm, crown prince of Prussia, and the latter for his brother Wilhelm, just as he was familiar with the architecture of Rheinstein Castle,[24] rebuilt by Lassaulx. Not content to take nourishment from German Romanticism alone, which could not help but attract a prince of Germanic origin, Eschwege was equally interested in Islamic architecture.

LEFT: Photographed at Pena by Antonio Novaes after a luncheon on April 3 1903, kings Edward VII and Dom Carlos I are with their family circle. Dom Carlos would be assassinated in 1908 with Crown Prince Dom Luis Felipe.

RIGHT: In the art-nouveau-style apartments of Dom Carlos is this statue of Louis-Ernst Barrias; *Nature Revealing Itself to Science* (1899). It stands out from panels painted by the king himself.

While waiting to visit North Africa, he found examples of the Islamic style in Sintra itself, at the *Palacio da Vila,* whose original structure was anchored in the Portuguese Gothic tradition.

Baron von Eschwege surrounded himself with such worthy collaborators as Nicolau Pires, who created the design and perhaps had a hand in the magnificent ink and watercolor elevations. Like the master stonecutter João Henriques, he was considered "one of the most practiced artists in the kingdom."

Earlier, the king had wanted only to restore and equip the old monastery. But, around 1840, it seemed desireable to build a new palace next to the ancient monastery, one that would be more comfortable and more in accord with royal dignity. Therefore in 1842, while the proud Clock Tower was being raised to replace the old building covered by a dome, new projects began to emerge. A brand new castle, worthy of the banks of the Rhine, rose (at least on paper) toward the sky with innumerable crenellated towers. These elegant, almost unadorned, designs, were to be extensively altered. The designs were executed, in large part, with Moorish influence and in the Manueline style, so that in the 1840s the castle became a strong component of the identity of the Portuguese nation. Doubtless motivated by aesthetic rather than political concerns, the modifications anchored Pena Palace in Portugal's prestigious past. Work continued until the death of Fernando in 1885. But the palace was habitable as of the 1850s.

The park created entirely out of an arid rock garden, from then on became a jungle where treelike ferns and a number of species of plants imported from Brazil, Africa, Australia, France, and Great Britain, thrived. The composer Richard Strauss once exclaimed: "Here is the true garden of Klingsor, and above is the Castle of the Holy Grail." In Europe during the second half of the nineteenth century, the magician Klingsor and the heroes of the old medieval legends had a plethora of choice in choosing their domiciles!

In this park there is an exquisite building, following the Romantic model of the English "Gilded Cottage" and it evokes a history of love. In 1860, at the opening of the lyric season of the São Carlos Theater in Lisbon, Dom Fernando fell in love with the beautiful Elsa Hensler, who was singing in Verdi's opera *Ballo in Maschera.* He had been a widower for seven years before becoming her lover, and he suffered the sarcasm of the press and disapproving whispers at court about his involvement with a singer or an actress! Whereas in Paris women of modest birth might slip into imperial alcoves without creating political upheavals, the affair created a scandal in Lisbon. But love triumphed. Named Countess of Edla by the grace of Duke Ernest II of Saxony, Fernando's cousin, Elsa became the morganatic spouse of the monarch in 1869. At Pena he built her the wonderful *Casa do Regalo,* better known as the Countess's Chalet. The chalet would be their favorite retreat. At the king's death, the contessa would inherit Pena Palace. Pena's chalet, destroyed by fire in 1995, remains only a memory.

The main entry to the new palace mixes Moorish and Manueline influence, with its extravagant arches and twisted columns imitating ropes.

BELOW: Detail of the postern. The motif of cannonballs is borrowed from a house in the *Bairro Alto* of Lisbon.

PRECEDING PAGES: The Portico of Triton (left) provides access to a vestibule decorated in extravagant raised ceramic tiles by the artist Cifka.

OVERLEAF: The exceptional lacy sculpture of the vaults and the tops of the columns is a display of Moorish stuccos in stone.

104

LEFT: Restored by Dom Fernando, the cloister of the ancient monastery has kept its sixteenth-century appearance, with arches supported by plainly cut stone columns. The ceramic tiles covering the walls are described in an order for twelve thousand tiles sent to Seville in 1512. In the center, a treelike fern has taken root in a giant shell held up by three tortoises.

OPPOSITE: This vaulted passage leads to one of the terraces of the palace.

OVERLEAF: Details of the Descent of Christ from the Cross and the Adoration of the Magi. Having miraculously survived the earthquake of 1755, King Dom João II and Queen Dona Catarina gave this grand marble and alabaster altarpiece to the Pena chapel. Dating from 1528–1532, this masterpiece of the Portuguese Renaissance was carved by Nicolas Chanterenne, a sculptor of French origin.

The extraordinary decor and trompe l'oeil in the Arab room was executed as of the autumn of 1854; the gray-colored frescoes are the work of the Italian Paolo Pizzi. Trunks of trees whose branches join at the vault evoke the naturalist basis of Gothic architecture.

OVERLEAF LEFT: The Indian room is one of the most imposing in the New Palace. It is furnished with carved teak seats imported from India. Finished under the direction of Domingos Meira, the stucco work boldly mixes Moorish and Asian inspiration. For this creation, Meira received the prestigious Order of Christ from the king.

OVERLEAF RIGHT: Seated in one of the courtyards of Pena Palace, her favorite residence, Queen Amelia of Portugal (1865–1951), born Princess of Orléans, daughter of the Count of Paris, is in the company of her son Dom Manuel and her favorite dogs. Dom Manuel ascended to the Portuguese throne in 1908 at the age of nineteen, following the assassination of his father and eldest brother.

PAGES 112–113: In the majestic Room of Nobility, Queen Amelia received visitors for tea. Despite its colossal dimensions, this room is particularly hospitable, its seats grouped in an informal manner instead of in a formal alignment against the walls. During Queen Amelia's time, green plants, cushions, and family photographs on the tables highlighted the pleasing disarray.

KAISERVILLA

KAISERVILLA

Emperor Franz Joseph I, King of Hungary

Empress Elizabeth of Austria, Queen of Hungary;

née von Wittelsbach

Ever since Franz von Wirer, personal physician to the imperial family, recommended the therapeutic properties of its salt and sulfur waters to his august patients in the 1820s, the town of Ischl has been a fashionable resort. Situated some thirty miles from Salzburg on the Ischl River, the little town was immediately adopted by the imperial family.

Its waters cured gout as well as what was then known as hysteria and hypochondria. The neighboring mountains of the Salzkammergut offered land famous for hunting. This region, one of the most picturesque in the northern Alps, took its name from the salt mines that were still in operation at the time, and which earned the royals that stayed there the nickname "princes of salt." A mere listing of the illustrious guests at Ischl, renamed Bad Ischl in 1906 thanks to the success of its baths, is dizzying. In 1828, Emperor Franz I came, and in the following year, Archduke Franz Karl and Archduchess Sophie, parents of the future Emperor Franz Joseph. In 1839, Empress Marie Louise, widow of Napoleon, in the 1860s, Empress Eugénie of France, King Wilhelm I of Prussia, future emperor of Germany, and Emperor Dom Pedro of Brazil; in 1869, Ulysses Grant, president of the United States of America; and, at the end of the century, Kings Alexander of Serbia, Dom Luis I of Portugal, Carol I of Romania, and Chulalongkord of Siam, all stayed there.

On August 15, 1853, the town of Ischl bore witness to an unusual stir. Archduchess Sophie was to meet her sister Queen Elizabeth of Prussia there. The young, handsome

emperor of Austria, who would soon be twenty-three years old, was supposed to join them to celebrate his birthday on August 18. But he was coming especially to meet the young woman who was chosen for his wife: Princess Helena, his German cousin, and the eldest daughter of Duke Max and Princess Louise of Bavaria. Rumor had it that a good horseman could make the trip from Vienna to Ischl in thirty hours. Franz Joseph, impatient to meet the young beauty that he would make an empress, on this occasion made the trip in only nineteen hours. Archduchess Sophie, called "the only real man in the Hofburg," was anxious to reinforce ties between Austria and her own family, which headed one of the most powerful Germanic kingdoms.

Now, the Bavarian princesses were late, and their trunks were even later. Hastily dusted off and combed, Helena, called "Néné," and her sister Elizabeth, "Sissi," were presented to the emperor. Sensible and dignified, the first sister had received the education of a future ruler. But it was the second sister, impulsive and timid, who charmed the emperor, to the point where he fell in love "just like anybody else." Questioned by her mother, Elizabeth answered, "How could anyone not like that man?" Only one shadow loomed on the horizon; the immense responsibilities of the future. "If only he were not an emperor!" she sighed.

At the grand ball given the next day, Franz Joseph danced with Elizabeth and honored her with all the bouquets destined for the other young ladies. Once he obtained permission from the king of Bavaria,

The imperial family photographed in 1860. Franz Joseph is standing on the left. Elizabeth is seated with her children. Next to her is her mother-in-law, the formidable Archduchess Sophie, reputed to be "the only real man" in the family.

Crowned by Neoclassical pediments, Kaiservilla (pages 114-115) looks down on an immense park at the foot of Mount Jainzen. The staircase of the villa (page 117) is decorated with numerous trophies of animals hunted in the mountains of the Salzkammergut, which were amply stocked with game.

MEDALLION (PAGE 116): Emperor Franz Joseph and Empress Elizabeth, in a portrait dating from 1854, the year of their marriage.

their engagement was celebrated, also in Ischl. The following Sunday, the blessing of the soon-to-be married couple took place in a jam-packed church.

Then came the moment of their separation and return to Vienna. The emperor confided to his mother, in a letter from Schönbrunn Palace dated September 6: "What a fall from the earthly paradise of Ischl to this existence of paperwork with its cares and worries." Elizabeth went back to the family estate of Possenhofen in Bavaria, her dear "Possi," whose four crenellated towers looked down on the Starnberg Lake. This was where the *Tristan*, a yacht belonging to her cousin Ludwig II of Bavaria, sometimes sailed. They were to find the king, drowned, in the same lake in 1886.

The rest is known: Her Royal Highness, Princess Elizabeth von Wittelsbach, duchess of Bavaria, age sixteen, became empress of Austria in 1854. According to custom, she made her solemn entry into Vienna in a golden carriage painted by Rubens and pulled by six white horses. The nuptials took place in the church where Maria Theresa married Francis of Lorraine, Marie Antoinette married the future Louis XVI, and Marie Louise married Napoleon by proxy. She had to familiarize herself with the strict court etiquette and with the Spanish ceremonial inherited from Charles V that she detested, and also had to withstand continuing remonstrance from her mother-in-law. Sophie chose as her daughter's first lady-in-waiting, a wrinkled *duenna* who kept close tabs on her—this for a young woman, who was so enamored of freedom, and who at Possi, had been surrounded by her favorite pets!

In 1853, Archduchess Sophie had purchased a country house in the Biedermeier style from a doctor who prescribed salt baths. It was the Villa Marstallier, in Ischl at the foot of Mount Jainzen. Metternich stayed several times in this house that a Viennese estate lawyer had built in 1834, and the archduchess gave it to her son as a wedding gift. An imperial escape, the future Kaiservilla would bear witness to a royal romance where, far from the worries of the court, Sissi could await the promise of more faraway journeys.

Soon the emperor undertook extensive work to lodge his future family and their large retinue. The bourgeois villa of fourteen rooms, once enlarged, became the central portion of the new Kaiservilla, onto which three perpendicular wings would be grafted, each decorated with a Corinthian portico with elegantly tapered marble columns. In this manner, the design of the villa took the shape of an "E" for Elizabeth. The architect in charge of the layout was Antonio Legrenzi, a brother of the young emperor's butler. Franz Rauch, architect of gardens for the royal and imperial court of Vienna, laid out the garden amidst undulating valleys, like an English park. He was aided by gardeners who came from the royal residences at Schönbrunn, Laxenburg, and the garden of Buda, on the right bank of the Danube.

The only concession to a more formal style was an ornamental basin of marble sculpted to portray groups of children playing with dolphins, in front of the principal facade in 1884. A bridge was built over the Ischl River to accomodate carriages, and a tunnel was dug beneath the park to hide the access road that went around the town. Enlarged

bit by bit, the estate extended from the river to Mount Jainzen, which became a part of it.

By the end of July 1854, the villa was again habitable. In August, it welcomed King Fernando II of Portugal as its first official visitor. In 1857, Rauch, who succeeded Legrenzi after his death in 1856, finished the building and the park. Other improvements would take place through the years, like the installation of electric light and heat, operated by a turbine powered by the Ischl River.

It was to Ischl and its rustically beautiful countryside that Elizabeth would go during times of sorrow. There, in June 1867, she mourned the emperor Maximilian, brother of Franz Joseph, shot in Mexico, and the Prince of Thurn und

Taxis, husband of "Néné." In that year, she made an effort to keep all threat of princely visits away from Kaiservilla, beginning with Ludwig II of Bavaria, engaged to her sister Sophie, whose strange behavior was irksome. Learning from the newspapers of the probable arrival of her aunt, the queen of Prussia, she even considered for a moment leaving town with regrets. Surrounded by dogs and horses, she liked a simple country life, long walks, and scaling Mount Jainzen, her "magic mountain," which put her ladies-in-waiting and her family very much to the test. Franz Joseph himself was very taken with this house that he called his "hunting lodge." In 1889, after the Mayerling Affair[25] and the enigmatic death of their son Archduke Rudolf, crown prince, it was again to Ischl that Elizabeth went to hide her despair, taking refuge in solitude. Dressed in black from that time on, she imposed a zone of isolation around the villa; she wanted no one to cross her path, not even the aides-de-camp of the emperor. In the park, the empress had Rauch build the Marmorschlossl (little Marble Castle), between 1856 and 1861. At the time modestly called "the cottage," this sumptuous building of Tudor inspiration, adorned with paneling, would welcome her at tea time. She put sixteen statues illustrating the legend of the *Nibelungenlied* above the picture railings.

In 1879, a new railroad track was built to allow the monarchs to go directly from Vienna to Ischl aboard the imperial train. A room was set up at the station to welcome them in a proper manner. It was in Ischl in 1889 that their daughter Marie Valerie became engaged to Archduke Franz Salvator, prince of Tuscany.

Modestly deemed "the cottage" as of the eighteenth century, the marble pavilion was built for Empress Elizabeth in the villa's park around 1856.

LEFT: A marble bust of the empress.

On July 16, 1898, Elizabeth left Ischl. Franz Joseph did not know it would be the last time he would see his wife. As a widower, the emperor remained faithful to his summer stays at Kaiservilla. The tall and stately silhouette of the hunter, dressed in his gray loden jacket and leather knickers, and wearing his green Tyrolean hat sporting a feather, was a familiar sight to the residents of Ischl. In August 1905, then again in 1907 and 1908, he greeted King Edward VII, distressed by the politics of Wilhelm II, who was strengthening the German fleet. In an attempt to please the British monarch who was staying at the Elizabeth Hotel, he agreed for the first time in his life to get into an automobile, an invention abhorrent to the public in the same way as was the telephone or the elevator.

A big celebration for the eightieth birthday of the emperor took place at Ischl in 1910. And on June 28, 1914, one month after the assassination of his nephew Franz Ferdinand at Sarajevo, it was from his study that Franz Joseph issued the proclamation *An Meine volker* (To My People) explaining to the empire his ultimatum to Serbia, to all effects and purposes the beginning of World War I.

When Franz Joseph died in 1916, his daughter Marie Valerie inherited Kaiservilla. Having renounced the throne along with her husband, she became a simple citizen of the Austrian Republic in 1918. The villa in that year celebrated its hundred-fiftieth anniversary and still belonged to a descendant of the illustrious House of Habsburg-Lorraine.

ABOVE AND OPPOSITE: The great room of "the cottage" is decorated in sumptuous Gothic style paneling. Sissi would come here to have tea, draw, and write letters or poetry. The statues placed on the delicately ornamented overdoors represent the heroes of the *Nibelungenlied* legend, dear to both the empress and her cousin Ludwig II of Bavaria.

OPPOSITE: Situated in the center part of the villa, in the great room on the first floor, are five large picture windows looking onto a terrace. During the empress's lifetime, this room was almost exclusively reserved for ladies. Franz Joseph received Empress Eugénie, widow of Napoleon III, here in 1906. Gilded mirrors, stuccos, bronzes, and porcelain vases recall the Louis XVI style.

RIGHT: The surface of this Italian pedestal table is decorated in micro mosaic, with a view of Saint Peter's in Rome, surrounded by medallions depicting the principal classical monuments of that city.

OVERLEAF: With its numerous photographs placed on the furniture or set in folding screens, the small study on the first floor recalls the family atmosphere reigning in the Kaiservilla at the end of the nineteenth century. When she became empress of Austria, Sissi discovered at Ischl the same atmosphere of freedom that she found in the castle of Possenhohen, or "Possi," of her childhood.

PAGES 126–127: The empress (right) was never so happy as when she was in the company of her horses and dogs, animals that her mother-in-law accused her of preferring to her own children. Here Franz Angerer photographed her around 1860 in the company of Horseguard, her favorite dog that a sculptor immortalized in marble.

123

In a corner of the emperor's study, the simplicity of the furniture in the private apartments is typical of the spartan taste of the monarch who slept in a simple cot at the Schönbrunn palace. From this modest study Franz Joseph reigned over his vast empire, during long and frequent trips to Ischl. His day began at 3:30 in the morning with a bath. Next came the examination of dossiers brought each day by special courier from Vienna. The uprisings of 1848 and World War I were among the rare events that momentarily deprived him of his dearly beloved residence. Despite appearances, the villa was equipped with modern conveniences. Since the end of the nineteenth century, it was lit by electricity and heated.

OPPOSITE: The washroom adjoining the emperor's study.

Photographed in August 1910, the emperor is dressed in his favorite outfit, a loden jacket and leather knee breeches, that he removed only to put on a military uniform. The patriarch, alone from then on, could never be consoled about the death of Sissi, assassinated in 1898.

PAGES 130–131: Huge display cabinets contain an exceptional collection of stuffed birds. Two stag heads and intertwining antlers plus a stuffed ibex are another reminder of the passion of Franz Joseph for hunting, the only distraction he allowed himself.

RIGHT: The emperor 's carefully arranged shotguns and (opposite) walking sticks seem still to be awaiting him.

MIRAMARE

A majestic fleet glided along in the Gulf of Trieste. It included the frigates *Novara* and *Bellone*, the finest jewels of the Austrian navy in the Adriatic Sea, the imperial yacht *Fantaisie*, six steamships, and even the French corvette *Themis*. All were decked with flags. On this sunny afternoon on April 14, 1864, Archduke Maximilian of Austria, younger brother of Emperor Franz Joseph, was preparing to leave Europe to go to his new empire of Mexico. This descendant of Charles V was the first in the thousand year-old line of Habsburgs to settle, albeit for a short and tragic time, in the New World. A small boat draped in red velvet trimmed with gold drew alongside the pier at Miramare Castle, where the Mexican flag was flying. Cannons from the *Bellone* joined by those from the *Themis* and those on the citadel of Trieste, announced the new emperor.

The Sunday before, Maximilian had received a Mexican delegation of conservative politicians who had come to offer him the imperial crown in the castle's reception room. Done up in his blue and gold uniform of vice admiral, he sat enthroned beneath a large embroidered canopy; at his side was his wife, Princess Charlotte of Belgium, studded with diamonds and radiant in her red velvet dress. Pale and solemn, he replied in Spanish: "With the help of the Almighty, I accept the crown from the hands of the Mexican nation that accords it to me." They had assured him an overwhelming majority would elect him—"by two Indians and a monkey," as the English would ironically comment. Franz Joseph had nevertheless warned him against assuming the throne of this distant country, which was under France's domination. Queen Victoria had even offered him

the throne of Greece as a consolation. But Franz Joseph's younger brother dreamed of an empire. At Miramare, bombarded with more and more urgent telegrams from Napoleon III, he finally took the throne. Charlotte was ecstatic.

On that day, taken with a sudden fever, Maximilian left the duty of presiding over the banquet in the hands of the new empress, and retreated with his doctor into the *Gartenhaus*, the park pavilion. Departure was rescheduled for April 14. Maximilian had to abandon his right to the Austrian throne in favor of his brother, who had come especially to Trieste. And he even had to renounce his much-loved domain of Miramare, which Franz Joseph took because it was heavily mortgaged. As Franz Joseph stated, What use would this castle be to an emperor of Mexico?

Finally the great day arrived. At two o'clock on April 14, the emperor and empress appeared on the marble steps leading to the castle. An orchestra struck up the Austrian, then the Mexican anthem, the latter recently composed in Paris; cheers resounded, flowers were thrown, handkerchiefs waved. A small boat took them to the *Novara*, where Maximilian locked himself in his cabin to weep. The destination was Veracruz, with a stop at Civita Vecchia in Rome to receive the pope's blessing. In the streets of the Eternal City, they were humming: "Beware, Maximilian / Return to Miramare/ The fragile throne of Montezuma / Is a French trap." Urged on by his wife, the very devout Catholic Eugénie de Montijo, Napoleon III had, in fact, set the whole thing up, to distract the United States, then in the middle of the Civil War.

137

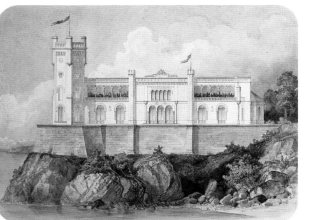

Two designs for Miramare Castle done in watercolor.

Despite modifications to the outside, the final design for Miramare remained faithful to the restraint of the architectural elevations. Their severity is in marked contrast to the warm luxury of the interior layout.

138   Born in Vienna in 1832, Maximilian of Habsburg was a tall, handsome blue-eyed man lost in a dream world. Unlike his older brother, the reactionary Emperor Franz Joseph, Maximilian had liberal ideas.

A brilliant vice admiral, he put the Austrian fleet back on its feet in the Adriatic. In Lisbon in 1852, he fell in love with Maria Amelia of Braganza, daughter of the deceased Dom Pedro, emperor of Brazil and king of Portugal. They became secretly engaged, with the approval of the dowager empress. Hardly back in Trieste, he learned at the beginning of the following year the tragic news of the death of his fiancée in Madeira. More than ever, he took refuge in his navy life. Happy to distance himself from his bothersome younger brother, Franz Joseph then offered him a mission to Albania.

In 1856, Maximilian was in Paris, asked by his brother to to feel out Napoleon III on the question of Italian unification. The archduke regarded the little man with the bearing of a circus master as vulgar. He thought "King Jerome"[26] resembled "a little Italian dentist," and that the empress Eugénie was of "an incontestable great beauty," however she enhanced it. He deplored the fact that "imperial dignity was totally lacking." During a dinner at the palace of Saint-Cloud, Maximilian made a good impression: "He really lacks only a chin to make him an accomplished gentleman," noted Fortoul, secretary of public education and religion.

Maximilian then went to Belgium by sea aboard the *Reine Hortense*, Napoleon III's yacht. He felt more at home in the court of Leopold I, who was from an old German family, the Saxe-Coburg-Gothas. Leopold's daughter Charlotte was a sixteen-year-old beauty, who had lost her mother, Princess Louise of Orléans, at the age of ten. Pedro V, king of Portugal, and Prince George of Saxony both courted her. Queen Victoria insisted to her "dear uncle" Leopold I that "Pedro would assure Charlotte's happiness much better than one of the countless archdukes" or even the prince of Saxony. Charlotte preferred the archduke. She therefore renounced a royal crown to marry him. On his return to Brussels in December 1856 for their engagement, Maximilian showed Charlotte the plans for the castle he was constructing in Trieste, that he baptized with the Spanish name "Miramar," quickly Italianized into "Miramare." He promised to add a chapel where mass would be said every day. She was under the spell. "He showed me my apartments, his, and the entire future plan of the castle . . . There will be a terrace with a fountain, and in the park, a Moorish kiosk furnished in Oriental style."

Erected on a rocky spur, Miramare is a massive structure of Tyrolean granite that commands the entire Gulf of Trieste. Entrusted to the architect Carl Junker, work on it began in 1856. The building is somewhat reminiscent of the Prussian and Rhineland castles that Schinkel built or restored, but it also bears a resemblance to the Sintra palace. Was this nostalgia for the Portuguese Pena palace, as the Sintra folly was also the work of a German? At Christmas in 1860, Maximilian and Charlotte moved into their lodgings on the ground floor. The ceremonial rooms on the second floor would not be finished until 1871. The luxurious interior decoration, studded with coats-of-arms of the Habsburg-Lorraine and

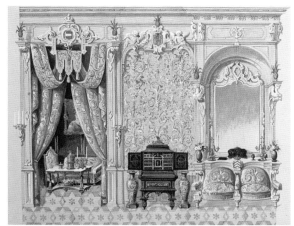

ABOVE: A design for the blue room's decoration, in watercolor.

CENTER AND BOTTOM : The library and Maximilian's study, called the Novara room; photos are from the Sebastianutti Studio, 1867.

PAGES 134-135: Built on a rocky point, the castle dominates the Gulf of Trieste.

PAGE 136:The grand staircase in Renaissance style, sculpted in massive oak, leads to the reception rooms. The pages' livery is embroidered with the coat of arms of Maximilian I, emperor of Austria at the beginning of the sixteenth century.

MEDALLION (PAGE 137): A photograph of Princess Charlotte and Archduke Maximilian by Braun, around 1860.

139

Saxe-Coburg-Gotha families, is largely the work of Franz and Julius Hoffman. A manufacturer from Lombardy specially wove the blue and red damask. For his bedroom with a lowered ceiling, Maximilian chose the simplicity of a ship's cabin. Likewise, in his study he reproduced the officers' quarters of the *Novara* instead of a rich Renaissance decor.

Designed by Junker, the English Park with winding paths could provide many surprises for the wanderer; streams, little lakes, wooded areas, and boxwood borders punctuated by marble vases. The couple took such frequent trips to the island of Lacrona on the Dalmatian coast, that they bought it and restored the old monastery. They were not aware of the legend promising a violent death to the island's owner.

In July 1857, the marriage of Maximilian and Charlotte was celebrated in Brussels, in the presence of Queen Marie Amélie, widow of Louis Philippe, and Prince Albert, consort of Queen Victoria. After a short stay at Schönbrunn Palace, the couple moved to the Villa Lazzarovich on San Vito Hill in Trieste, while they waited for Miramare to be finished. Charlotte exclaimed, "In the north, they have no idea what a really blue sea looks like."

Named Austrian viceroy of Lombardy and Venice, Maximilian succeeded the sinister and horribly repressive Count Josef Radetzki. In Milan, the young couple resided in the royal palace and there they were humiliated by the local nobility who, far from being won over, would send their servants to performances over which the viceroy presided at La Scala instead of attending themselves.

LEFT: Miramare Castle in 1860, taken by Alois Beer, photographer of the Austrian court.

RIGHT: A portrait of the Empress Charlotte taken by Angerer in Vienna in the 1850s.

OPPOSITE: Two views of the park, the flowerbeds (top) and the pergola (bottom), bordered by exotic plants.

140

Only merchants attended a ball given by the viceroy. Nevertheless, efforts to gain the sympathy of the Italians made Prime Minister Cavour uneasy: "He is the only one who can wreck the plans for Italian unity." Franz Joseph, also irritated at the liberal designs of his brother, took government of the Italian provinces away from him in 1859. He felt it would be better to have the police state back! The Austrian defeats at Magenta and Solferino presaged the loss of Lombardy. To his surprise, Maximilian even lost his command of the Austrian fleet. Humiliated, he decided to devote himself to the decoration of his castle at Trieste, but soon, sadness invaded life at Miramare, and the couple took separate bedrooms, perhaps owing to Maximilian's infidelities. Carlotta—as she liked to be called in Italy—was chomping at the bit. Gone was her initial enthusiasm; she admitted preferring a life filled with duties to "contemplating the sea on a rock until the age of seventy." Under the circumstances, the Mexican adventure seemed a blessing to her, despite the warnings of Leopold and Queen Victoria.

Once in Mexico, Emperor Maximilian missed Miramare. When he commissioned the restoration of the Chapultepec residence on an admirable site in Mexico City, he asked his secretary: "Do you think this place could be baptized Miraval, just like I called my castle in Trieste Miramare?" He did not know that he would never again see his beloved rock in Italy.

The empire was a failure, and fell apart when the French emperor, Napoleon III, was forced to withdraw his troops. Leaving her husband in Mexico, Carlotta left for Europe to plead his cause. To save Maximilian's throne, she set sail for Veracruz on July 13, 1866 aboard the steamship *Impératrice Eugénie*. In Paris, an interview with Napoleon III was disastrous. She and her husband needed money and an army. "The Empress of Mexico came here and almost knocked down the door of His Majesty's office," wrote Prosper Mérimée. "I don't think she got what she wanted." As a last resort she requested an audience with the pope. Received with all pomp and ceremony in September [27], she forced open the doors of the Holy Father.

On January 16 1868, the frigate *Novara* docked at Trieste, this time carrying a catafalque draped in black velvet embroidered in silver. The imperial boat berthed at Miramare, with the mortal remains of Maximilian on board; he had been shot on June 19, 1867 at Querétaro, far from home.

Charlotte was now unaware of everything. She had lost her mind. They locked her up in the *Gartenhaus*, where the windows were screwed shut. Starving, she lived in terror of being poisoned. After great difficulty she had arrived in Trieste, accompanied by her brother, Prince Philip, count of Flanders and she left Trieste for Brussels for good by special train after the body of the ex-emperor had been returned to Europe. She died in 1927, far from the "really blue" sea, in Bouchout Castle, whose lugubrious towers are reflected on the lake. During World War I, German authorities posted a sign on the park gates there: "This castle is inhabited by H.M. Empress of Mexico, sister-in-law of our revered ally, the Emperor of Austria."

OPPOSITE: Maximilian had his
study decorated to look like the
officer's quarters at the stern of
the warship *Novara,* pride of the
Austrian fleet, once he became
vice admiral in 1854. A great
admirer of English ships, whose
comfort and neatness he
appreciated, he wrote, "The
English, intelligent as they are,
know that the more pleasant life
aboard is for officers and
midshipmen, the more they like
their ship, and the more
easily they endure time spent
away from home."

RIGHT: Maximilian's library is
enriched by seven thousand vol-
umes and decorated by busts of
poets.

The small dining room was the main room in the private apartments belonging to Charlotte. It is hung in light blue damask woven in Lombardy, and decorated with a pineapple motif, symbol of abundance, and with a crowned anchor, an allusion to Maximilian's rank of vice admiral. This same material was used in the bedroom (opposite) where a neo-Gothic *prie Dieu* from Vienna can be seen. A hidden door permitted the archduchess to go directly to the chapel that Maximilian had built for her of his own design, fulfilling a promise he made before their engagement.

OVERLEAF: On the second floor of the castle, the Chamber of Princes is decorated with richly sculpted woodwork and inlaid with exotic woods. Unfinished when Maximilian left for Mexico, this room contains portraits of his ancestors.

LEFT: The Audience Hall is furnished with lacquer and gilt Venetian chairs and setees. In the Chamber of Reigning Princes (opposite) , the monumental canopied bed—undoubtedly of Italian origin—was a wedding present to Maximilian and Charlotte from the French emperor Napoleon III.

OVERLEAF: The Conversation Room, covered in red damask woven with crowned eagles, has overdoors painted by Giuseppe Pogna from Trieste; they show Maximilian's favorite places and have sumptuously sculpted frames.

Archduke Maximilian always had an ingrained taste for the exotic. Before living at Miramare, he had a room in the Villa Lazzarovich in Trieste decorated in the Moorish style that he later transferred to the *Gartenhaus* of Miramare. At Miramare, he created Japanese and Chinese rooms, each of them used as smoking parlors. The porcelain collection, sculptures, and small furniture in the Chinese room (opposite) are reminiscent of the extremely refined atmosphere of a little study in Schönbrunn Palace that was dear to the Empress Maria Theresa.

OVERLEAF: The throne room is the largest in the castle. Its ambitious iconographic plan celebrates the glorious house of Habsburg. It is an irony of history that Maximilian, who dreamed of reviving the empire of Charles V, died before achieving it.

FERDINAND I.

PIERREFONDS

PIERREFONDS

Emperor Napoleon III of France

Empress Eugénie of France; née Maria-Eugénie de Guzman,

Countess of Teba

As soon as he was proclaimed emperor of France in 1853, Napoleon III left the Elysée Palace to move to the Tuileries. The new court, which he wanted to be dazzling, revived the practice of the *ancien régime* and the First Empire of luxurious seasonal migrations. There were courts at the royal residences in Paris, Saint-Cloud, Fontainebleau, and Compiègne. To these were added other private residences: the castle of Villeneuve-l'Etang and the Villa Eugénie at Biarritz, where men could come "sans culotte" (without breeches), that is without their court attire of silk stockings and black pants.

Passionately interested in archaeology, the emperor wished to restore a feudal castle as a holiday place. Fascinated by the restoration of the ramparts at Carcassonne successfully directed by Eugène-Emmanuel Viollet-le-Duc (1874–1879), he quite naturally consulted this architect. Viollet-le-Duc suggested rebuilding the imposing ruins of the Castle of Coucy, in Aisne, an enormous fortress of the fourteenth and fifteenth centuries that in his eyes reincarnated the ideal medieval castle. The emperor's choice fell finally upon Pierrefonds, closer to Compiègne, where restoration promised to be less expensive.

Situated on a promontory overlooking the forest, a little town, and a lake crossed by the Berne brook, the castle had been erected in the 1390s by Louis of Valois, duke of Orléans and brother of King Charles VI. It is incontestably the most attractive of the medieval ruins of the Ile de France. Worthy of the illuminated miniatures of castles in the *Très Riches Heures du duc de Berry*,[28] the fortress successfully resisted several sieges in the course of the Hundred Years War. An attack in

1616 by Louis XIII's army was fatal. Its towers were razed, and its enormous outside walls were ripped open down to the foundation. In 1810 Napoleon I had the state purchase this romantic ruin that Corot later painted.

Considered at best an "upstart," European royals balked at addressing Napoleon III (who was an elected emperor) as "brother," as was the court custom, in their correspondence. It was certainly not by chance that Napoleon III chose for his residence this medieval castle linked to the royal estate where Joan of Arc had gone, nor did he choose the place simply because of its archaeological interest. The castle was allied to the oldest European monarchies as well as to Christianity, and medieval architecture conferred on it the aura of a place for the idealized knight. The noble stones added a respectable patina to a new French heraldry that was too flashy. The iconography of the interior decorative program seems to confirm Napoleon III's intention; a painting that runs all around the emperor's bedroom represents the deeds of a knight in the fourteenth century. In the empress's bedroom, which is vaulted with diagonal ribbing as in a chapel, the mantle of the vast fireplace is painted with the eight knights of the Round Table, surmounted by King Arthur in effigy.

Viollet-le-Duc was an appreciated guest at the Tuileries palace. Son of a former governor of the palace under Louis-Philippe, he actually lived there longer than the monarchs themselves. He particularly endeared himself to Empress Eugénie, who called him "my good man Viollet" or "my dear violet flower."

160 He also oversaw, in collaboration with the architect Lassus, the decoration of Nôtre Dame in Paris for the marriage of Napoleon III and Eugénie de Montijo in 1853, and once more for the baptism of the imperial prince three years later. According to Prosper Mérimée's instructions he also designed Mademoiselle de Montijo's coat of arms. He planned the decoration aboard the special train given to the monarchs by the Orléans Railroad Company, ornamenting the paneling and ceilings in a profusion of painted ivy, wild roses, morning glory, roses, and poppies. When the contest for the new Opéra in Paris started, eventually won by Charles Garnier, Viollet-le-Duc was the candidate of the imperial couple. When the building of an imperial palace was planned in Algiers, one that was never to be built, Viollet-le-Duc was also chosen. With the exception of the sculptor Carpeaux, who also frequented the Tuileries, he was the only great artist of the time to be admitted to the court and to be readily welcomed into the intimacy of the imperial family.

During trips to Compiègne of the court, his wit, his good company and his multiple talents were much appreciated. These traits in turn made him an acerbic caricaturist (he did not always show his cartoons, which were sometimes cruel, to the parties concerned), and a brilliant scenery designer, indeed a prompter for intimate performances in the little theater built for Louis-Philippe. His longtime friendship with Prosper Mérimée, inspector of historical monuments, and a more than intimate friendship with Madame de Montijo, the empress's mother, made

him even more beloved at court. If she did not share the emperor's taste for archaeology, Eugénie did see Pierrefonds as a wonderful added attraction for their son, Prince Louis-Eugène Napoleon. And when she suddenly left for the waters of Schwalbach in 1864, in protest against the infidelities of her husband, she traveled as the Countess of Pierrefonds; she would use this alternate title several times until the end of her life.

At the beginning of 1858, Viollet-le-Duc submitted two different designs for renovation of Pierrefonds. The first showed "the complete view of the restored castle, so that His Majesty could have an idea of the whole, which might be rather sad." More audacious and less costly, the second project proposed only "the rebuilding of the central tower in the middle of the picturesque ruins," a tower that, "situated on a culminating point where the view is beautiful from all sides, could make a very nice residence." To tantalize his patron, Viollet-le-Duc painted the imperial couple in a seductive gouache, having coffee like any middle-class couple in a Gothic room made cozy by curtains and sumptuous rugs. It seems the second design was accepted and work began immediately. But, bit by bit it was modified, and the restoration of several towers was added to the initial work. Finally in 1862, the emperor decided to reconstruct the entire castle; the building site then employed as many as three hundred workers. In the following year, Napoleon III decided to furnish the castle and asked the architect for more detailed interior designs. Viollet-le-Duc wrote to his son on November 18, 1863:

"H.M.[29] . . . wants to finish the whole castle in a rather short time. I've been asked to furnish it."

Along with hunting in the forest of Compiègne and social distractions, visits to the work site at Pierrefonds were among the required amusements of the court during stays in the neighboring Compiègne palace. Viollet-le-Duc, who, along with Mérimée, was one of the essential hosts of the famous "gatherings" at Compiègne, guided the visits. Started in 1856, the "Compiègnes" gathered together groups of several people at a time, invited to spend a week during the months of November and December. They would meet writers like Sainte-Beuve, Dumas-fils, Flaubert, musicians like Gounod and Verdi, and scientists like Pasteur. A special train awaited the privileged guests at the *Gare du Nord*. After getting off the train at Compiègne, court carriages took them to the palace. Including the court, royal personnel, and a large number of domestics, the palace hosted up to nine hundred people. There was a "serious" gathering with state officials and government secretaries, an "elegant" gathering,

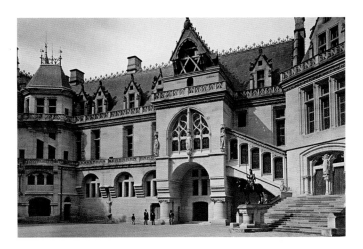

which required six additional carriages for baggage, and an "artistic" gathering. Carefully preparing her guest list, the empress sighed, "It's a problem of choosing cabbage, the goat, or the wolf."[30]

Excursions to Pierrefonds were taken in a surrey. In a letter dated October 23, 1861 to the countess of Montijo, Eugénie's mother, Mérimée recounted an incident that happened at Pierrefonds in the presence of the king of Prussia, Wilhelm I, and about a dozen others: "The gardener woman (a mistress of the emperor), noticed a big stone lizard coming out of the roof and asked what it was. —It's a gargoyle —What is a gargoyle? —It's a pipe to conduct water from the roof to the outside. —What! They took the trouble to make something like this as a plumbing system? Why, it must have cost a lot of money! —Yours costs a lot more, replied Maréchal Vaillant,"[31] the secretary general of the emperor's household. In his *Journal* Count Horace de Viel Castel revealed that the name of the "gardener woman" was Countess Walewska, who was disgraced.

Cats decorate the dormer windows, and along with elephants, monkeys, chimerae, and other whimsical animals, they make merry in the sculpted decor of the castle. These as well as the famous sixteen-and-a-half-foot-long "lizards" (which are in fact salamanders) constitute one of the most captivating creations of Viollet-le-Duc at Pierrefonds.

In 1867, when Paris attracted all of Europe to its World's Fair, Viollet-le-Duc received a certain Count von Berg to Pierrefonds, in fact, Ludwig II of Bavaria. Did this visit reinforce his desire to build his own Gothic castle?

Viollet-le-Duc rebuilt the road (left) that follows along the surrounding wall. A Romantic recreation of a medieval fortress, Pierrefonds mixes dream and erudition.

BELOW: Empress Eugénie in her riding outfit, with the crown prince, her dear "Loulou," photographed in 1864. During numerous escapades that she made at this time to distance herself from her unfaithful spouse, the monarch traveled incognito as the countess of Pierrefonds.

This is more than probable. Nevertheless, the work led by Viollet-le-Duc is in no way comparable to Neuschwanstein. Pierrefonds, with its surrounding outer walls equipped with eight towers, encompassing imposing authentic remains and containing a mixture of archaeological references and inventions in the interior court, is as faithful as possible a restoration of a medieval castle. But Neuschwanstein is a frenzied imitation that grew to the dimensions of a dream. Behind its high stone walls, Pierrefonds certainly conceals an authentic medieval structure. Therefore, Viollet-le-Duc chose to create a series of metal frameworks for support. The one he made for the chapel was admired at the 1867 World's Fair before it was set in place in the castle. However the restored castle maintains a certain coarseness and medieval brutality that was unique in Europe at this time.

In 1870 when the Franco-Prussian war broke out, the castle was still not habitable. Seeking refuge in Britain at Hastings after the proclamation of the Republic on September 2, Eugénie thought for a while of moving to the Villa Vicentina in Trieste that Princess Bacchiochi willed to the crown prince. Did the ghost of Maximilian, emperor of Mexico, for whom she wore mourning during the festivities of 1867, dissuade her from moving there? More than twenty years afterward, she bought some land on Cape Martin to build the Cyrnos Villa. Fascinated by the tragic destiny of "Elizabeth of Austria," Eugénie declared, "This will be my Achilleion," (where Elizabeth sought solitude). She too lost her son, the crown prince, who was killed in Zululand in 1879.

In the Honor Court, a low gallery (left) runs along the base of the large residential area where the ceremonial rooms are located, contrasting with the severe lines of the architecture. Capitals and gargoyles (below and opposite) translate the brilliant whimsy of the architect.

OVERLEAF: Designed by Viollet-le-Duc and sculpted by Perrin, enormous salamanders (left) recalling the fabled Middle Ages take out rainwater from the Honor Court. Overlooking the corner landing of the grand staircase (right) and the chimera of Fremiet, Saint James was put there by Napoleon III's architect.

168

OPPOSITE: In a reception room, the furniture and paneling show the extent of Viollet-le-Duc's talent as a decorator. The large bench with its tipped-up back is sculpted in leafy foliage. Its gracefulness announces the art nouveau style. This chimera biting its wing (left) brings the fantastic bestiary of the cathedrals to the palace apartments.

A length of more than 154 feet makes the Hall of Valiant Damsels the largest in the castle. It was to serve as a location for imperial balls. Barrel vaulted in the shape of a ship's hull, it has an opulent painted and sculpted decor.

PAGES 170-171: During the Second Empire, this room, photographed by Mieusement around 1868 was made to showcase the magnificent collection of medieval armor belonging to Napoleon III. The colossal fireplace (page 171) is surmounted by statues of the Nine Valiant Damsels, heroines linked to the literature of courtly love. Inspired by the Valiant Knights of the Castle at Coucy, this sculpture gallery is the "Gothic" version of a famous painting of Winterhalter. Here Empress Eugénie is represented as Semiramis, legendary queen of Babylon, surrounded by her ladies-in-waiting.

LEFT: Statues of Charlemagne and his paladins (left) flank the door of the Room of the Valiant Damsels.

A sumptuous octagonal vault reinforces the similarity between the empress's bedroom and a chapel. The stylized tree painted on the mantle of the fireplace (left) holds the eight knights of the round table within its branches. The stenciled decorations on the walls and vault (left and opposite) here attain their apogee.

PAGES 174–175: In the emperor's bedroom, the fireplace lintel is sculpted with golden bees strewn on a red background with several amulets and bears the motto: Qui veult, peult ("He who wants to, is able to"). A symbol of hope, the bee had first been chosen by Napoleon I as decoration for his imperial robes.

AJUDA

AJUDA PALACE

King Luis I of Portugal

Queen Maria Pia of Portugal; née Princess of Savoy

Some royal residences have a fortified castle, a monastery, or else a simple hunting lodge as a predecessor. Ajuda Palace, in Belèm near Lisbon, was born of a miracle and two catastrophes. Its direct predecessor was a wooden shack.

According to a sixteenth-century account, a shepherd found a miraculous statue of the Virgin Mary in a grotto here. Soon the faithful rushed to implore the Virgin's help (*ajuda* in Portuguese). Then on November 1, 1755, a terrible earthquake reduced Lisbon, "the Queen of the Tagus," to dust, along with all its artistic treasures born from the colossal riches of the Empire of the Indies. King Dom José I deemed it more prudent to transfer his residence and court to Ajuda. Much earlier, João V had planted flower and vegetable gardens there, hoping to build a summer palace, which was in fact never built. For more than thirty years, the Portuguese court had to be content with a simple wooden house, the *Real Barraca* or *Paco de Madeira*, until a day in November 1794 when fire completely destroyed the building. As a result of this new disaster, and an act of the Regent Prince Dom João, a new palace, this time in stone, emerged.

Conceived in a baroque style that by then was out of fashion, the first design was not accepted, and its author was ousted in favor of the architects Francisco Xavier Fabri and José da Costa Silva. Some new designs were drawn up, more in line with the neoclassic aesthetic that was sweeping over Europe. Financial and political difficulties and the departure of the royal family for Brazil following the French invasion of 1807 significantly slowed progress at the work site. When the royal family returned in 1821, the palace was far from completed. A new architect, Antonio Franciso Rosa, was hired. At Ajuda Palace in 1828, three states met to proclaim Dom Miguel the absolute monarch, consequently removing his niece Doña Isabel Maria from the throne and causing a terrible civil war. When she was once more proclaimed queen in 1834 under the name Isabel II, and married Duke Auguste-Charles de Beauharnais of Leuchtenberg the following year, the future of the palace finally seemed to be certain. In fact, her future husband decided to finance the completion of the western facade of the building. But fate intervened again; Dom Augusto died the following year. Work proceeded at a chaotic pace, punctuated by several official ceremonies like the *baisemain* (hand kissing) of the queen and other court celebrations.

Upon the remarriage of Doña Isabel to Ferdinand of Saxe-Coburg-Gotha, the palace that was burdened with sinister memories was abandoned for the Palacio das Necessidades; and in the summer, for Pena Castle at Sintra. Conceived as a baroque palace at a time when a look inspired by classical antiquity was triumphing, built and decorated in a pompous classical style until the middle of the 1840s while the Romantic aesthetic was in full swing, Ajuda seemed an unappreciated architectural monster. It was a huge, stiff palace perfect in symmetry, with interminable facades pierced by hundreds of identical windows. The "royal shed of boards" as of the seventeenth century gave birth to a royal barracks.

Ajuda Palace, painted in watercolor by Enrique Casanova in 1889. The facade was influenced by that of Buckingham Palace in London. The first stone was laid on November 9, 1795. The palace hesitates between Tuscan elegance and neoclassic sobriety (pages 178–179). A sumptuous chandelier in crystal and gilded bronze is in the king's study (page 181).

MEDALLION (PAGE 180): Dom Luis I surrounded by his wife Doña Maria Pia and their children; oil on canvas by Joseph Layraud, 1876.

BELOW: Dom Luis I in his navy uniform, photographed in 1889, the year of his death.

It was during Holy Week in 1862, that the new king Dom Luis decided to move into this residence. Having suddenly lost his three brothers the year before—among them King Dom Pedro V—he welcomed a distance from the Palacio das Necessidades, where sad memories haunted him. Finally, Ajuda would become a royal residence!

But the somber palace needed to be redone from top to bottom. While the exterior kept its architectural layout, the ceremonial rooms and private apartments were entirely decorated in the alluring and abundant style of the 1860s. Imagine an igloo lined in silk, on the scale of Versailles!

The new queen, Maria Pia of Savoy, daughter of the king of Italy, Vittorio Emmanuel II, would remain a step ahead of the renovations when she named Joaquim Possidonio Narciso da Silva (1806–1896) as primary architect of the royal house. Finding herself in a palace as excessive as it was uncomfortable, in the midst of a court whose ancient customs she was unaware of, this fifteen-year-old monarch chose the offensive. Previously excluded from the restoration of the Pena Castle by Dom Fernando, how did Da Silva take the personal intrusion of the empress's supervision of his layout? Described by her daughter-in-law, Princess Amélie of Orléans as "very distinguished in her imperious physical demeanor," Maria Pia did not lack flair. The arrival of modern comforts in Ajuda, notably in the form of bathrooms adjoining bedrooms, running hot and cold water, and even toilets did nothing to lessen her desire to create a place worthy of the splendor of the monarchy. Enriched by a profusion of stucco and trompe l'oeil paintings, the ceilings were ornamented with hundreds of crystal chandeliers, each one weighing, it is said, more than a ton. The windows were draped in Swiss lace, thick velvet, or silk damask. The parquet floors were inlaid with precious wood.

Sumptuous wedding gifts arrived from the old and the new worlds, including vases from the Sèvres manufacturer and China. The queen's trousseau contained an abundance of silver plates, to which were added countless items ordered from the most famous establishments in Europe. The firm of Paul Sormani in Paris, reputed for its luxurious copies of Louis XV and Louis XVI marquetry furniture or Chinese lacquer work, was a large supplier. From ceramics richly set in gilt bronze, to Louis XV style furniture in in undulating *rocaille* highlighted by gilded bronze mounts, or from fireplaces of Gothic or Renaissance inspiration, emerged an opulent decor that was so confident it could have been in World's Fairs, where cabinetmakers, decorators, bronze and ceramic artists demonstrated their virtuosity. Replacing the former interior vestibule of the palace, the winter garden's walls and ceilings were entirely covered with a facing of richly veined chalcedony, a gift of the viceroy of Egypt. In the throne room and the ballroom, immense Aubusson carpets were laid down.

Blond and pale, endowed with a sweet look and a "melancholy face" Dom Luis was himself an amateur artist and unparalleled collector. A painter and musician

FROM LEFT TO RIGHT: Three watercolors by Enrique Casanova—the Telegraph Room, the King's Painting Studio, in neo-Gothic style, and the Blue Room. Commissioned by the queen, these watercolors, bound in an album, were destined as a birthday gift for Dom Luis on October 31, 1889. But the king died on October 19.

BELOW: Dom Luis, Doña Maria Pia, and Crown Prince Dom Carlos, two months old, by F. A. Gomes, photographer of the royal family, 1863.

with a respectable baritone voice, he was also a fervent reader of French literature and regularly corresponded with Victorien Sardou, the revered author of *Tosca*. At the Ajuda Palace, the king had a workshop set up in the "artist" style reminiscent of certain houses in the *plaine Monceau* district in Paris. Is the Gothic-inspired woodwork that covers this room as well as the adjoining library more evocative of the banks of the Rhine than the Tagus? Could it have been an acknowledgment of the king's father, Dom Fernando's, taste? Was the latter full of advice about this apartment where the somber oak veneer contrasted with the eighteenth-century inspiration of the other rooms in the palace? That is very probable.

Very little is known about the daily life at Ajuda, except that mornings were generally spent in the intimacy of family life in the apartments dispersed all along the east wing and spread out over the wooded gardens. The family played music, painted, and sculpted. The queen entertained herself by doing watercolors and receiving tradesmen. After the death of Dom Luis in 1883, Maria Pia continued to live in Ajuda Palace, although at a slower pace, with her younger son, Dom Alfonso. Created to administer the finances of the widowed queen, the newly established Household of the Queen looked after problems from then on. A register kept in the private secretary's office mentions, in particular, bicycle rides, and impulsive yet comfortable picnics, with tents to protect the guests from the wind. There were chairs, tables, porcelain plates, and silver flatware to temper a picnic's rustic character. Nevertheless, ponderous court etiquette was forgotten here. There were also trips to the summer cottage in Sintra, to Pena Castle, or to the picturesque bathing spas at Ericeira, where the little fishing port abounded in crayfish. It was from this place in 1910, following the proclamation of the republic, that the royal family embarked for Gibraltar.

In May 1886, beneath a shining sky, Ajuda Palace bore witness to the wedding of Dom Carlos, Duke of Braganza, to Princess Amélie of Orléans, daughter of the count of Paris. Greeted by salvos of cannons and bugle blows, the procession of court carriages was a dazzling sight. Drawn by white mules clad in silver, the carriages of the royal family dated from the eighteenth century.

184

For the occasion, Queen Maria Pia put on a sky blue velvet dress, copied from Maria de Medici's in a Rubens painting from the Louvre, strewn with "cascades of pearls and sprays of diamonds." On her royal blue mantle, white silk pomegranates replaced the fleur-de-lis of Rubens' model. In her high-collared dress of white silk (worn over velvet) and a long veil of old lace, the bride-to-be held a book of hours bound in ivory, a gift of the ladies of the department of Seine-Inférieure in France. There was a great ball at Ajuda Palace, then a bullfight on the *Capo de Sant'Anna* Square, and finally fireworks on the banks of the Tagus were the conclusion to the festivities. Despite their magnificence, the celebrations at Ajuda maintained an informal tone; everybody danced until the early hours and the king, himself a cellist, willingly joined in with the orchestra.

Unusual for the courts of Europe, the palace was periodically open to the public. In 1876, the *Diario de Noticias* attested to the success of the visits: "The people flocked in such great numbers that during the two first hours, they needed to be organized into groups of 100 to 300 people. It was estimated that 7,000 or 8,000 people came there." In October 1910, after Doña Maria Pia's departure into exile, Ajuda Palace was closed. Transformed into a museum in 1938, today it remains permanently open to the public. Deprived in the first decades of the 20th century of hosting historic court events to show off the splendor of court life, today the palace's sparkling setting is used for selected ceremonies of the president of the Portuguese republic.

RIGHT: The Oak Room, that served as a smoking room for the king and his guests, was separated from the ladies' Blue Room by an immense picture window.

OPPOSITE: During court receptions, the king liked to come into a room that was devoted to chamber music, singing, and playing the cello. Placed on the rug, his instrument bears the autograph of Emile Mennesson, "called Guarini, stringed instrument maker of Rheims," and dated 1882.

OVERLEAF: Redecorated in honor of the marriage of Dom Luis I and Maria Pia of Savoy in 1862, the Winter Room received a coating of chalcedony, presented by the viceroy of Egypt. This vast room boasts gilded wood furniture; at its center is a marble fountain. In the Saxon Room (pages 190-191) the curious furniture is ornamented with Meissen porcelain. Hung in pink satin, her favorite color, the room served as an antechamber for the private apartments of Queen Maria Pia.

In the queen's bedroom, a surprising *prie Dieu* of rosewood highlighted by an ivory Christ, a wedding gift to Maria Pia, was made by Giuseppe Martinotti and Luigi Figlio, cabinetmakers from Turin. The seat is hidden in a double-door cabinet inlaid in mother of pearl. The furniture, of veneered ebony was ordered from the Parisian company, Krieger-Racault Successeurs. The walls are covered with oil or photographed portraits of the royal families of Italy and Portugal (below and opposite).

Dating from 1880, the portrait of Queen Maria Pia is signed by Carolus-Duran, a French artist who painted the glorious people of the Third Republic as well as foreign grandees.

The queen's boudoir still has its silk covering from the 1880s as well as its original floral motif carpeting. Ernesto Condeixa painted the over doors with mythological divinities. The striking reclining chair, draped in velvet (right), is embellished by silk embroideries with Maria Pia's monogram surmounted by the royal crown. Practically abandoned until the marriage of Dom Luis and Maria Pia in 1862, Ajuda Palace became the favorite residence of the new queen. Made king in 1889, her son Dom Carlos allowed her to continue living there and he moved to the Palacio das Necessidades.

The Room of the Initials L. M. is named for the ceiling decoration that mix the monogram of King Dom Luis and Queen Maria Pia in the middle of allegorical compositions. Here the heavy tints and the original trimmings have been preserved, and are typical of the "tapestry style" of the second half of the sixteenth and seventeenth centuries. Woven in silk wool and cotton, the velvet is probably of French origin.

OPPOSITE: The former king's study has recently been restored according to a watercolor from 1889. Original fragments permitted the foliage wallpaper to be remade in our time. The large Sèvres vase presented to Dom Luis by Napoleon III represents illustrious personages from the sixteenth and seventeenth centuries.

PAGES 196–197: Ajuda Palace was not spared the fad for chinoiserie born around the middle of the eighteenth century. Hung in English silk, the Chinese room's ceiling is in the form of a tent. In 1866, the Portuguese artist Procopio painted Asian motifs on the doors in gold on a red background. Large porcelain vases from the nineteenth century complete the decor.

In the library, next to the painting studio (pages 200–201), it is believed that there is influence of the design of King Fernando, father of Dom Luis. Two warriors in medieval costume support the fireplace lintel. The furniture is sculpted with life-size carvings in Venetian baroque style; below is a detail of an armchair.

PAGES 200–201: Views of Dom Luis's painting studio. Situated on the second floor of the palace, this room of neo-Gothic inspiration is decorated in sculpted oak paneling, made by the woodworker Leandro Braga (1839–1897). Auguste Moreau signed the bronze grouping of two children.

The immense throne room in the south pavilion. The consoles and large neoclassic mirrors were placed here during the reign of Dom Carlos (1889–1908). Beneath a red velvet canopy, the monarchs' thrones (of which a reflection can be seen on the right in the mirror) are sculpted with the Braganza coat of arms, held by two cherubs. They are inspired by Italian baroque furniture.

OVERLEAF: The banquet room is still used for official receptions by the President of the Portuguese Republic. In the nineteenth century, musicians sat in the gallery on the second floor, where the marble statue of the poetess Sappho, by Francesco Confalonien, can be seen (right). In 1903, King Dom Carlos commissioned the lacquered chairs in white and gold for an official visit of King Edward VII to Ajuda.

NEUSCHWANSTEIN

210 Neuschwanstein is a castle in the clouds, born out of the engagement of a lake and an imperious rock. The "New Rock of the Swan"—this is its literal translation—thus replaced the "High Land of the Swan," Hohenschwangau (pages 36–59), the family castle situated below. Powerful harmonies and the brass and percussion of a Wagner orchestration drown out the mellow chamber music of the paternal residence. Haunted by the memory of *Tannhäuser* and *Lohengrin*, Ludwig II of Bavaria first called upon a theater decorator, Christian Jank, to make a preliminary design for what was to become the most striking of all the buildings he undertook. It was most important to fix the parameters of the dream; the architecture would come later. Thus, from its very conception, the castle was placed under the aegis of fiction and illusion: "I am not afraid of appearances," retorted the king, disdainfully sweeping away with a wave of his hand the gossip about him from the Munich court. "If I need to, I will have them created." The castles he built show that he was a master of illusion.

Built on the Bertzenkopf, an almost inaccessible rock at a height of almost 3,280 feet, Neuschwanstein looks like a mineral concretion, a fantastic stalagmite attacking the sky. In a letter to Wagner, Ludwig expressed his enthusiasm: "The spot is one of the most beautiful imaginable. It is sacred and inaccessible" Sacred and inaccessible, just like the king who, little by little, walled himself up in his dreams of absolute monarchy, in the solitude of mountains inhabited by phantoms of old Germanic legends.

The unerring choice of site, the genius of the location is part of the magic of all the residences of Ludwig II. To build Herrenchiemsee, where the Sun King's Versailles was cre-

ated anew, King Ludwig chose the arid island of Herrenwörth on the melancholy Chiemsee. For Königshaus, the royal residence of Schachen, Ludwig had a wooden house transplanted from the banks of the Bosporus to a wild ridge without any vegetation, where access could be gained only on foot or horseback. For Linderhof Castle, a white rococo jewel, he chose a river of green flowing down from the high valley of Graswang. In May 1867, during a visit to Wartburg Castle, built near the grotto where, according to legend, Tannhäuser lived with Venus, the king immediately conceived the idea of building his own medieval fortress. At first it was only a matter of restoring some feudal ruins looking down upon his beloved Hohenschwangau. These were remnants of the fortifications that used to defend this strategic site at Vorderhohenschwangau, the highest point, and at Hinterhohenschwangau, from down below. The present castle's enormous mass joins these two sites and simultaneoulsy swallows them up. One of the paradoxes of the medieval dream is that it indeed leads to the ruin of rare surviving vestiges.

Invited in the same year (1867) by Napoleon III to the World's Fair in Paris, Ludwig II was impressed by a visit to the building site at Pierrefonds, where he was guided by Viollet-le-Duc. Ludwig was in the company of Princess Pauline von Metternich, another great Wagner enthusiast and the wife of the Austrian ambassador to France. "He never stopped envying the big toy constructed in heavy stone," wrote Jacques Bainville. However, rather than procuring the help of a Bavarian equivalent of Viollet-le-Duc, Ludwig took an opposing track.

212

The first designs were somewhere between picturesque hideaways for plundering knights and late Gothic *burgs*, whose jigsaw gables were reminiscent of the old town of Nuremberg. The final design adopted a more barren style for the exterior. Nearby Wartburg Castle evoked the Grail Castle, the legendary fortress of Montsalvat where knights kept the chalice of the Last Supper containing the blood of Christ.

To render the silhouette of Neuschwanstein more tantalizing, borrowings from military architecture of the thirteenth to the fifteenth centuries were added, such as machicolations, a sentinel's watch, a postern, and watchtowers. Work was first given to *Hofbaudirektor* (Director of Court Buildings) Edouard Riedl; then, around 1872, to the chief architect for royal buildings, Georg von Dollmann, who had, at the time, just finished the rococo folly of Linderhof Castle. Von Dollmann, in turn, gave control of the site to Julius Hoffman in 1884.

The cornerstone of the building was laid in 1869. Construction began on the *Torbau* (postern) where temporary lodging was arranged for the king so he could survey the site. A steam engine brought construction materials to the summit of the rock, which afterward was accessed by a new road. In the year 1879 alone, accounts reveal the use of 930 tons of marble from Salzburg; 9,100 tons of sandstone from Nürting; 1,200 tons of cement, and 400,000 bricks. All this was a colossal expense, which would be surpassed only by the cost of the "Versailles" of Herrenchiemsee. The relationship between the king and his architects and contractors was sometimes strained. He declared to a servant: "It has always been thought that the most arrogant animal is a king. Now I who am a king, affirm that there is an animal even more arrogant than a king, and it's a contractor." From the heights of Saüling, to the west, is where the castle offered its most spectacular perspective. It was a fantastic piling up of towers, gables, pepperboxes, and pinnacles worthy of an old Rhineland *burg*, and dreamed of only with the pen and ink of a Victor Hugo. In the winter, this bigger than nature building block toy dominated the fog that whitened the waters of the Alpsee. Flanked on the north by the lodging for knights, and on the south by a building of more modest proportions reserved for women, the gigantic royal residence immediately made room for a grandiose *sängersaal* (singer's hall) inspired by Wartburg Castle and built in honor of Wagner.

Ludwig II constantly harassed the artists. Here such and such detail of armor had to be modified because it did not conform to what he thought was historically accurate; there such and such scene had to be completed as a Good Friday scene, because legend called for it. On the other hand, it did not matter that the paintings profusely scattered about the walls, were the work of mediocre talents. The only thing that counted was the stories in the immense tapestries that surrounded visitors. Blond, athletic heroes in golden armor fighting monsters worthy of the "tunnels of horror" in our amusement parks, and robust virgins with long tresses, cinched in gleaming metallic corsets, seem to jump out of an end-of-the century picture made as historical paintings.

Had he lived long enough for Ludwig II to meet him in Paris, Delacroix himself would not have obtained a commission to do the Neuschwanstein murals, because the king did not want "paintings of quality." He wanted beautiful images to incite the dreams of good little children thanks to their loud colors, stereotyped characters fixed in declamatory gestures, with carefully designed foliage that looked like color plates in encyclopedias.

A "sanctuary of wonders," according to Empress Elizabeth, the throne room, with its striking mosaics, is as beautiful as a Byzantine church. A throne of ivory and gold, protected by a richly embroidered canopy, was supposed to be created instead of the main altar. It was never built. Six canonized kings can be identified on the mosaics in the apse, among them Saint Louis of France, whose effigy also decorates the Oratory of the king. Made king by the grace of God—at least he thought so—Ludwig II finally identified with divinity itself. But the tabernacle of the new cult remained empty.

While Neuschwanstein was slowly rising up from its rock—too slowly for him—Ludwig II was already thinking about other buildings, not in Bavaria but on faraway islands like Crete, Cyprus, certain Greek Islands, the Canaries, and Madeira. His impatience was worthy of that of his cousin Sissi who got tired of Corfu almost as soon as her palace of Achilleion was finished. In 1872, then again in 1875, if the report published by the parliamentary commission charged to depose him is to be believed, the king sent the superintendent of state archives, Franz von

Loher, on a mission to these places to provide an exact description of them. The project is supposed to have failed because of an inability to assure royal control over the chosen spots. Barely a king anymore, Ludwig II was consequently condemned to exercising his dream of majesty inside the borders of his own country. At the time of his death in 1886, Neuschwanstein was still a giant work site full of scaffolding. Only the basic framework and a part of the interior were finished. Work ceased in 1892.

On June 9, 1886, a commission to depose Ludwig was sent by Prince Luitpold. Upon arrival in Hohenschwangau, an alarm set off by a coachman immediately sounded in Neuschwanstein. Defense of the castle was mounted. Volunteer firemen, police on foot or on horseback, mountain men and villagers, groomsmen, and all the servants that for years were Ludwig's only companions, were ready to give their lives to save him. The emissaries of Prince Luitpold escaped the popular fury but were locked up in the guardhouse, and only freed later. On the night of June 11, male nurses with government approval finally seized the king and transferred him to Berg Castle. He demanded, in vain, a key to the highest tower of Neuschwanstein, threatening to throw himself from it. But he had to say good-bye to the palace peopled with ghosts. The dream born at Hohenschwangau ended; he had to face reality.

In Starnberg Lake, a cross marks the spot where, on June 14, the king's body was fished out, not far from that of the psychaiatrist, Dr. Gudden, who used to accompany him on his walks. The day before, he had telegraphed to

LEFT: Portrait of Ludwig II of Bavaria dressed in the Grand Order of Saint George, by Georg Schacninger. Inspired by the great royal French portraits of the seventeenth and eighteenth centuries, this painting was finished in 1887, a year after the king's death.

RIGHT: An unfinished drawing for Falkenstein Castle by Christian Jank, who made a gouache from it in 1883. Even before Neuschwanstein was finished, Ludwig II was dreaming of an even more fantastic building. A theater designer, Jank also made the first designs for Neuschwanstein.

214   Munich: "Here everything is going marvelously well, beyond words." On his body was evidence of struggle and strangulation.

The writer Ferdinand Bac provided Paul Morand with another version of the final act confirmed by the Empress Eugénie. On the evening of Ludwig II's death, Empress Elizabeth of Austria was waiting for him in a carriage on the shore of the lake. Maurice Paléologue also affirms that during that tragic night, Elizabeth hastened from Ischl, finding herself on the opposite shore of Starnberg Lake, in Feldafing. Author of the *Livre de raison d'un roi fou (Book of the Reasoning of a Mad King)*, the writer André Fraigneau dared to put words in the mouth of the king. He said, "Ariane, my sister, could have predicted that Theseus was a doctor and that he would have overcome the Minotaur with a straitjacket. But, we are giving the lie to a fable. I will come out of the Labyrinth . . . you will take me to Achilleion that you had built, in moving ignorance of its true destiny."[33] But in place of the lemon trees and the stone beds in Corfu, Ludwig II would know only the mud bottom of Starnberg Lake.

ABOVE: In the grotto of Linderhof Castle, Ludwig II is represented as a swan knight, like Lohengrin.

OPPOSITE: Ludwig II purchased the Moorish Pavilion at the Paris World's Fair in 1867 and situated it in Linderhof's park. Three peacocks, their tails encrusted in Bohemian crystals, surmount the throne in the form of a couch. The stained-glass and colored-glass lamps bathe this Asian daydream in an unreal light.

Covered in mosaics with a gold background worthy of a Byzantine church, the throne room of Neuschwanstein Castle was bereft of the throne that never would be made. Weighing almost a ton, the immense gilded brass chandelier (page 217) had to be raised and lowered with a winch. Completed by Wilhelm Hauschild, as was the entire decor of this room, the painting beneath the cupola represents Roman law, symbolized by Emperor Augustus. This enormous throne room appears to be a pathetic attempt by Ludwig II to affirm his sovereignty. In his eyes, he had been ridiculed by the parliamentary regime, and then again in 1870, humiliated by the unification of the Reich under the scepter of a Prussian, Wilhelm I, whom he hated. He declared in 1868 to M. de Cadore, the French minister in Munich, "Mr. Bismarck wants to make a Prussian province of my kingdom. He will succeed. Alas!" Cut in Austria, the floor mosaics (right) represent stylized flora and fauna.

OVERLEAF: An immense golden sun darts its rays onto a blue cupola studded with stars (left). For lack of funds, the columns in the gallery on the second floor had to be painted to resemble lapis lazuli (right). The apse is decorated with a Christ in Majesty, surmounting the effigies of king-saints punctuated by palm trees.

219

Thanks to the intricate richness of its paneling and enormous furniture, and the abundance of its paintings, Neuschwanstein appears to satisfy Ludwig's desire to be better than Hohenschwangau, to surpass the family castle in dreamlike power and splendor, as an ultimate homage to Richard Wagner, his beloved friend. Covered in dark oak sculpted paneling, Ludwig II's bedroom (left) harbors the most extravagant furnishing in the castle: the king's bed, surmounted by an enormous canopy crowned with pinnacles. Painted by J. Frank on a slab of gilded copper, an effigy of the Virgin and Child watched over Ludwig II as he slept. Woven by the House of Jorres in Munich, the hangings, with backgrounds of royal blue—Ludwig II's favorite color—are decorated with the coat of arms of Bavaria and the lion of the House of Wittelsbach. The murals depict the legend of Tristan and Isolde.

OPPOSITE: A detail of the spectacular earthenware stove in neo-Gothic style, an indispensable alternative to hot air central heating.

OVERLEAF: Painted to look like tapestry, the decoration of the great room relates the legend of the Holy Grail and the story of Lohengrin, the swan knight with whom Ludwig II identified throughout his life. The over door represents Lohengrin leaving the Grail Castle aboard a skiff pulled by a swan. Through this door (left) Ludwig II could enter the Venus Grotto, with its artificial stalactites, leaving Lohengrin to find Tannhäuser. Defined by four marble columns banded with gilded metal and by blue hangings embroidered with the legendary birds, the "Swan's Corner" (right) was one of the favorite retreats of the king, who loved to read there.

The fifth-floor vestibule leading to the Room of the Master Singers, was painted by Wilhelm Hauschild to depict the legend of Sigurd and his quest for the treasure of the *Nibelungenlied*. This room, which, along with the throne room, is the largest in the castle, takes inspiration directly from Wartburg Castle where in the thirteenth century, the singing contest took place, later put to music by Wagner in *Thannhäuser*. It was after a visit to Wartburg that Ludwig II imagined this room.

OPPOSITE: A strange sculpted palm tree guarded by a dragon supports the starry vault over the staircase that leads to the king's apartments on the fifth floor. Thought up by Ludwig II, the pillar symbolizes a desire to transcend earthly life and all its imperfections, to attain the divine sphere and eternal peace. A second staircase located above the palm tree goes up to the spire of a tower that is about 223 feet high.

226

PELES

From Bucharest to Sinaia, the "Pearl of the Carpathian Mountains," the traveler crosses the desperately monotonous plain of Valachia to struggle up the foothills of the Transylvanian Alps. The trip presents a gripping contrast. "In a little more than a hundred kilometers you pass from China to Savoy," wrote Paul Morand. Immediately after being elected prince of Romania, Charles of Hohenzollern-Sigmaringen took his first trip to Sinaia in August 1866. Sinaia, which takes its name from the Monastery of Sinai, founded on this spot at the end of the seventeenth century by the *spatar* (sword-carrier of the reigning prince) Mihail Cantacuzène, is perched on the mountain to the north of the capital city. The prince was attracted, as was his wife, Elizabeth, née princess of Weid, by the wilderness aspect of the Carpathian mountains, and by the Peles, a capricious stream, which has etched an uneven canyon into the rock. He decided to establish a summer residence at the foot of Mount Furnica, on the granite foothills that overhang the Valachian Plain and the Prahova Valley. In the midst of reconstruction, Bucharest at that time was only dust and noise. The monarch had come to Sinaia seeking pure air and the mountain light, which takes on pink and blue hues with the passing hours.

Famous throughout Europe under the pen name Carmen Sylva, Princess Elizabeth confided to the stream, out of which she sometimes saw a sprite emerge, "Contemplate, for a while, my dear Pelesch, that they are planning to build a big castle on this very spot. . . . Imagine, they are going to destroy the rocks, take out the forest, and it is you who will have to saw down the poor trees that they cut down into

pieces." To the monarchs, this admirable landscape recalled memories of their German childhood. After persuading Maximilian of Habsburg to accept the imperial crown of Mexico, it was again Napoleon III who suggested a German prince, Charles of Hohenzollern-Sigmaringen, for the Romanian throne. When he became prince of Romania, Charles sententiously declared, "Divine Providence has decreed that a Hohenzollern shall reign over the fountainhead of the Danube, and also shall reign at its mouth," slightly redoing the map of Europe in the process. His reign marks the birth of modern Romania. Freed from Turkish oppression after the victory of 1877, Romania was finally recognized by all of Europe as a kingdom in 1881. The prince then became king of Romania under the name Carol I. Morand tells of the "joyous entry" of the prince into Bucharest, his capital city in 1866. He stopped in front of the ancient dwelling of a *Boyar*,[34] which became the princely palace, after having housed a barracks and a hospital. "Carol I, scratching his big eagle's nose, asked for help in the midst of the confusion: 'So where is the palace?'" He could have said, Morand adds, "So where is my capital city?"

An ancient barracks was not worthy of a descendant of the more than 800 year-old illustrious House of Hohenzollern. So, while awaiting the construction of the royal palace in Bucharest, Carol I would have not a castle but a *burg* perched on a Carpathian mountain. This building that eventually from afar resembled an arrogant city, bustling with towers and pinnacles was given the name *Castel Peles*. The fantastic pile rose up in the light of the moon, like "The

231

232

Carpathian Castle" imagined by Jules Verne in 1892, brushed by pairs of white-tailed eagles emitting their dreadful cry.

The prince requested plans for his new residence from Wilhelm von Doderer (1825–1900), a professor then director of the *Polytechnikum* of Vienna. Author of designs for the Vienna arsenal, architect of the army headquarters, and also of the Mehadia Baths, then in Austria-Hungary, Doderer was doubtless brought to the attention of Carol I because of his military architectural experience. Did the king intend to rule his architect with an iron hand? Having a very good idea of what he wanted, he radically modified Doderer's design. From the beginning of the construction, it was evident that the true architect of Peles was the prince himself. It was he who pointed out the documents from which the architect would be inspired.

Models of the *Castel* were mainly German, drawn from imposing fortresses like Sigmaringen, restored in the nineteenth century, or Coburg, with walls as high as cliffs and picturesque towers crowned by slender cones. Evidence of military architecture remained in the former provinces of Valachia and Transylvania, such as Braun Castle, constructed after 1382. The colorful, vivid alternation of facades in freestone and patches of wood and masonry, inspired by civilian architecture of the Middle Ages, and was compatible with the monarch's vision as well as his purse. A castle entirely of stone would have cost much more.

Not content merely to suggest models, Carol also personally directed the work when time permitted. He was seen bravely mounting the most rickety scaffolding, beneath the uneasy gaze of Princess Elizabeth. The latter described the work site as a veritable Tower of Babel combining idioms from all of Europe: "Italian and Romanian masons are working on the foundation, Bohemians work as day laborers, Albanians and Greeks excavate the stones, the carpenters are Germans and Hungarians, Turks bake the bricks. There are Polish foremen and Czech stone cutters. The French design and the English measure. . . . Fourteen languages are spoken here. Men sing, curse, and quarrel in every dialect. It is a noisy, amusing mixture of men, horses, cattle, and buffalo." The first stone was laid on August 22, 1875. During the following year, the king fired Doderer. His talents had been mainly used to create the castle's foundation. His replacement was Carol's former assistant, Johannes Schultz, who was younger and more easily controlled.

The official dedication of the palace took place on October 7, 1883, but work continued from 1893 until 1914, under the direction of the Czech architect Karel Liman. In 1911 he created, in place of an interior courtyard, the fabulous Hall of Honor, reminiscent of the splendor of the Rothschild family palace in Vienna. He also erected the small Pelisor Castle where, beginning in 1903, Ferdinand of Hohenzollern, nephew of Carol I, and his wife, Princess Marie, daughter of the Duke of Edinburgh and the Russian Grand Duchess Maria-Alexandrovna resided. When she became queen after 1920, Marie asked him to restore and equip Braun Castle.

LEFT: Queen Elizabeth and King Carol photographed around 1914.

RIGHT: The Austrians Gustav Klimt and Franz Matsch painted the decorative panels in the Little Theater of the castle. It was in this room, in 1906, that the first movie in Romania was shown.

The concert room photographed around 1910. Furnished in 1906 in the English Renaissance style, it is paneled and covered in Cordovan leather. An avid musician, Queen Elizabeth received such great artists as Ignace Paderewski and Pablo Sarasate at Peles.

In addition, two other architects, this time French, would work on Peles. André Lecomte du Noüy and Jean Ernest who, after having collaborated with Liman, would be commissioned in the 1930s to maintain the buildings. In *De Pontoise à Stamboul (From Pontoise to Istanbul)*, which appeared in 1884, the writer Edmond About delivered an enjoyable account of the castle's dedication. He described "the paradoxical village of Sinaia," without peasants and "much more worldly in appearance and in reality than Bougival or even Trouville."[35] Since the king moved his summer residence there, the villas, the elegant summer houses, even the castles multiplied. Rug merchants solicited visitors of distinction to purchase rather colorful carpets, but unfortunately they were, "less beautiful and twice as expensive as [those] from Caramania."[36] Peasant women who had textiles and embroidery in gaudy colors to sell, drew this cry from Edmond About: "Woe to the Orient if this great colorist allows fuschia and indigo blue in his work!" In Sinaia, there were two rival hotels, one next to the other, and one could go for lunch to one and for dinner to the other. One of the two belonged to a former servant of the house of the king. The authorities, to protect him from competition, found the equal distribution of lunch and dinner unfair.[37] When he arrived at the former monastery where the princely couple resided, awaiting completion of their castle, the writer raised his eyes. "Five minutes afterward, we discovered above our heads the elegant and bizarre silhouette of a building such as we never saw except in our dreams or in illustrated fairytale books. It is a palace-

234

chalet where the most knowledgeable archaeology and the most modern whimsy seem to juggle with wood, marble, glass, and metal. Between the towers and turrets, which pierce the skies, uniforms can be seen glistening on the balconies covered with verandas." Leo Bachelin, King Carol's librarian, commented diplomatically on the castle's composite character as worthy of extravagant "villages" that different nations were raising at the World's Fairs in Paris, London, or Vienna. "If it is true that the architecture of the mountains is the chalet, and that of rock is the fortified castle, then it can be said that Castel Peles, which started out as a fortress and ended up as a chalet, has married these two elements in very fortunate combination."

The ceremony to dedicate the castle began with the blare of military music. French guests were struck by the contrast between the very imposing, martial presence of Carol I and the group composed of the queen and her ladies-in-waiting, who were dressed in traditional Romanian costumes and coiffed in large white veils embroidered with motifs in vivid colors. Later, in a room "almost as large and high as a church" where the guests sat "in sculpted wooden stalls like canons in a choir," the queen played the piano accompaniment for a young Romanian singer from a good family. Here the rigid etiquette of the European courts had no place. The musical soirées at Peles were famous

throughout Europe. George Enescu and the great Romanian poet Vasili Alexsandri later became frequent guests. Patroness and friend of artists, Elizabeth received musicians, writers, and painters at Peles, great personalities such as Pierre Loti, Sarah Bernhardt, Réjane, Ignace Paderewski, and Pablo Sarsate.

Peles today surprises the visitor by its excess, just as it surprised foreign visitors at the end of the nineteenth century. They discover a monument without equal in Europe, born in a country ravaged by incessant conflict, by cholera, and cut off by Russia from two of its provinces in 1877. Edmond About cited the sum of three million French francs for the building dedicated in 1883, and noted that at that time the budget of Romania, which amounted to one hundred twenty million francs, hardly sufficed to maintain the army. A state secretary had to content himself with 1,200 francs per month. He omitted saying that the colossal sum came partly from the personal cache of the king, not only from the citizens. The residence, built from 1873–1883, cost around 6.5 million Romanian gold lei, with a total cost reaching 16 million lei in 1914.

Sick yet certain of the victory of his native land, Carol I did not survive the refusal of Romania to enter into World War I on the side of the Germans and Austrians. He died in September 1914. Peles had just been completed.

With its picturesque facades where frescoes alternate with sections of carved wood, the interior courtyard of the castle (left) evokes the square of a German town in the Middle Ages or Renaissance. Seen from one of the windows of the castle (right), the effect is even more striking. This style recalled memories dear to King Carol, a descendant of the illustrious Hohenzollern-Sigmaringen family, and to Elizabeth, herself of the lineage of the princes of Wied. This architecture also had the advantage of being much less costly than a building in stone.

OVERLEAF: Two views of the castle's vestibule, whose architecture emphasizes the richness of the marble.

238

The castle's outstandingly
luxurious interior decoration—the
work of Viennese and German
artists and artisans—was directly
inspired by the German Renaissance.

OPPOSITE: Karel Liman, a Czech
architect, equipped the Hall of
Honor in 1911. Personally involved
in the architectural conception of
the castle, King Carol himself
furnished architects with the
models from which they took
inspiration. The unusual spiral
staircase is a copy of the one in
the Bremen City Hall.

RIGHT: The grand staircase
leading toward the great hall.

OVERLEAF: The Hall of Honor seen
from the gallery on the second
floor; on the wall is a series of
eighteenth-century Aubusson
tapestries. Inspired by German
models, the stained-glass
windows of the antechamber
(page 246) depict picturesque
roughneck soldiers in armor and
plumed headdresses. Finished in
1906, the armor room (page 247),
paneled in oak, boasts an exceptional horse and rider, dating from
the sixteenth century.

243

Equipped with latches of mannerist inspiration and busts of winged women, the windows are inlaid with authentic fragments of Swiss stained glass from the Renaissance that bear the emblem of each canton.

OPPOSITE: The Heynmann Studios in Hamburg did the king's study in 1883. This firm became famous at the London World's Fair of 1851.

The silver coffer from Napoleon's time, is stamped with the hallmark of Christofle in Paris.

Invited to the dedication of Peles, the novelist Edmond About wrote about the decoration of the castle: "A veritable profusion appears on the woodwork: several rooms, and not the smallest ones, are worked from top to bottom like a Renaissance sideboard." A corner of the council room (left) one of the last rooms to be finished before the castle was completed in 1914, is a perfect illustration of the writer's remarks.

OPPOSITE: According to a vow of Queen Elizabeth, who made a career as a woman of letters under the pseudonym Carmen Sylva, the former music room was transformed into a parlor in 1905. The woodwork is surmounted by paintings of Dora Hitz illustrating the fairy tales and German legends put into verse by Carmen Sylva. It was here that the queen held her literary soirees. The Maharaja of Kapurtala presented the sculpted teak furniture (pages 250–251) to the Romanian monarchs as a gift.

LEFT AND PAGES 254–255: Conceived by the French architect Charles Lecomte du Noüy, the long, rather than wide, Moorish room is decorated with examples of Asian weapons. This room dazzled Pierre Loti, who attempted to recreate the splendor of mythic Asia in his own house in Rochefort. The walls and ceilings are covered in stucco that has been gilded and painted in the Spanish-Moorish style. An Islamic style fountain of Carrara marble completes the decor.

OPPOSITE: The Turkish smoking room is hung in silk embroidered with golden thread. Despite its gleaming couches, glittering copperware, and scimitars rendered harmless by their transformation into pieces of furniture made by the Viennese House of Seigert, this is not an import from Istanbul. Without the authentic collection of Turkish Persian vases, which completes the ensemble, one might be tempted to see an attempt to emulate a hereditary enemy in this choice!

ACHILLEION

Between Hungary and Cape Martin, Madeira and Ireland, Algeria and Switzerland, between the Bavarian lakes and the Aeonian Sea, the empress Elizabeth of Austria led an errant life. She fled Vienna, the court, and even the emperor. She forgot her duties as a mother, a wife, and an empress, and felt no constraint. The person who Maurice Barrès called "The Empress of Solitude" was only really at home on a boat. She was empress of the wind, Our Lady of the Sea, a solitary idol carried along by the waves. She loved storms and had herself tied to the mast of a ship to better enjoy their spectacle. Or perhaps, like Ulysses resisting the call of the Sirens, she preferred to be attached so as not to succumb to the temptation of the waves unleashed. Leaving, always leaving for "over there." On her yacht the *Miramar*, she had one of the quarter benches enclosed in sailcloth. Seated in this, her "Isolde's tent," she could see nothing but the sea.

The imperial yacht was luxurious and simple. According to Constantin Christomanos, who was one of the empress's Greek teachers, the cabins reserved for her "had the special character of a sailor's lodging." The seats had white dust covers under which "no silk could be seen." But there were flowers everywhere. On the bridge was a pavilion with windows framed in blue silk and in the center was a circular couch that provided a panoramic view of the sea. Salt water was drawn by crew members aboard a rowboat to provide the empress with her daily bath. She compared sailing to being on an island where all disagreements and troubles were banished. It was "an ideal life, chemically pure, crystallized, without desire or consciousness of time." On a voyage the important thing is not reaching the destination but the trip itself, a parenthesis suspended in time and space. Achilleion at Corfu was an indissoluble link to the dreams of a "chemically pure" life.

In 1861, aboard the royal yacht *Victoria and Albert*, reserved for the use of the queen of England, Elizabeth discovered Corfu after a trip to Madeira. The climate did wonders for her, as she suffered from a pulmonary illness. This island, looking out on the snowy tops of the Albanian Mountains in the distance, dazzled her. She bathed in the sea, sat on the beach surrounded by her dogs, and contemplated the moonlight. The *Iliad* became her bedside reading.

In 1885 she embarked on a long sea voyage aboard the *Miramar*, wanting to see the important archaeologist Heinrich Schliemann's work site at Troy. Again she returned to Corfu, where the Austrian consul, Baron Alexander von Warsberg, a distinguished scholar of Greek who served as her guide, charmed her. In 1887, accompanied by von Warsberg, Elizabeth set out to retrace the footsteps of Ulysses to Leucadia and Ithaca, but came back again to Corfu. She learned ancient and modern Greek. The following year, greatly affected by the death of Duke Maximilian of Bavaria, her father, she set off again for Greece, whose beauty he had shown her. On the return trip, she stopped once again at Corfu, where the writer Vraila received her. On her return to Trieste and Miramare Castle, where Emperor Franz Joseph came to meet her, she let him know about her plan to build a villa at Corfu. Von Warsberg would be commissioned to direct the work and arrange the garden.

261

LEFT: The dining room of Achilleion in 1891, with chairs that were later taken away by Emperor Franz Joseph to the Kaiservilla in Ischl, where they were photographed (far left).

PAGES 258-259: Erected at the request of Emperor Wilhelm II, the bronze statue *Achilles Victorious*, by Johannes Götz, looks down on Achilleion's terrace

PAGE 260: The marble bench where the empress mourned her son.

MEDALLION (PAGE 261): A statue to the memory of Elizabeth, commissioned by Wilhelm II.

262

Elizabeth purchased the Vraila Villa and in its place created a building evoking "a royal castle and the happy time of the Phaiacians," inhabitants of ancient *Kerkyra* (Corfu) where the shipwrecked Ulysses was greeted by the beautiful Nausicaa. In 1889, devastated by the tragic death of her son Rudolf at Mayerling, flight and trips were more necessary than ever to comfort her soul. A confidential note addressed to the plenipotentiary ministers and ambassadors of Austria-Hungary stipulated that the empress wished to receive no more happy wishes, the word "happy" having lost all meaning for her.

At Corfu, construction progressed, directed since the death of von Warsberg in May in Venice by the Italian architect Raffaele Carito. Then, at the end of 1890, it was overseen by a naval officer, Baron August von Bukovich. Finished in 1891, this eclectic building with white facades, porticos, and terraces, linked the mysteries of Pompeii with the comfort of villas on the French Riviera. The empress stayed there seven times, in spring or in autumn, until 1896.

The imperial boat would take Elizabeth to a white marble dock where a smiling marble dolphin awaited her: "See over there, my laughing philosopher is the first to receive me" she would say. The crowned dolphin, which appears among the many decorative elements in the palace, became the emblem of Achilleion. Dressed entirely in black, carrying a white parasol, the empress would climb up the marble steps to the terrace of her residence, brushing past olive trees, cypresses, laurels, and flowering lemon trees. She chose Achilles, the handsomest and bravest of the heroes of the Trojan War, as the protector for her residence. In 1892, the Austrian artist Franz Matsch painted the grand staircase, which depicts Hector's conqueror Achilles pulling his dead body behind a chariot. She had a marble statue, *Achilles Dying* by Ernst Gustav Herter (pages 282–283), placed in the garden. She had already commissioned a version of it for the park at Miramare Castle, where, after her brother-in-law Maximilian's death, she frequently resided. Trieste was the port city that connected her to Austria.

The agony of the hero no doubt took on more tragic meaning after the death of her son Rudolf at Mayerling. At Corfu, Elizabeth had a funeral monument erected to his memory. The emperor Franz Joseph would later have it transported to Vienna. Still surviving in the garden today, is the marble bench where the empress mourned Rudolf.

The interior decor of Achilleion is as eclectic as its facades. If the grand staircase flanked by bronze statues of Zeus and Hera (pages 272–277) is a masterpiece of Pompeiian influence, the dining room, with its little stucco angels, recalls Bavarian rococo. In the chapel, inspired by the first Christian basilicas, a statue of Our Lady of the Guard, protectress of sailors watches. The empress purchased it in Marseilles.

On the other hand, the garden was placed under the protection of Olympic gods and classical heroes. Four marble gods—Aphrodite, Artemis, Apollo, and Hera—guard the staircase that leads up to this enchanted domain, where silhouettes of cypress and palm trees look down on it.

ABOVE: Of baroque inspiration, the stucco in the dining room breaks with the program of Achilleion as a palace of classical antiquity. The vestibule (above right) as seen in a photograph of 1891.

With its red and white columns and its capitals in blue and gold, its bronze lamps hung from chains, the Peristyle of the Muses (pages 278–281) transports us to Pompeii, in an ancient dream heralding *Gradiva* (1903), Wilhelm Jensen's novel immortalized by Sigmund Freud's analysis.

It has been said that some of these statues came from the Villa Borghese. There, feminine beauty is honored; the Three Graces—Leda seduced by Zeus who changed into a swan; a dancer of antiquity, for which, according to Canova, Pauline Borghese may have posed; the courtesan Phryne—all praise the perfection of the body and a lack of concern of the soul. Olive trees with winding trunks, witnesses to a thousand-year-old landscape, perfect this odyssey across the bounds of time.

Elizabeth could not stand being cloistered at home. During a trip to Corfu, she told Christomanos: "We will spend as little time as possible in the house. We must not spend the precious hours of our lives between walls unless we have to, and our lodgings must be such that they can never destroy the illusions that we bring back each time from the outside." Then, in 1893, she informed the emperor that she no longer liked Achilleion. She once said: "If they make me stay somewhere, even paradise, it would become a hell to me." She wanted to sell it and give the proceeds to their daughter Marie-Valerie and her "large family." Distressed at the thought of new wanderings, Franz Joseph answered that they would starve, "even if you sold your house."

264

RIGHT: Recently restored, the dock at the end of which a marble dolphin always greets visitors.

OPPOSITE: The Peristyle of the Muses in 1891, photographed by Borri and Sons of Corfu. These columns and multicolored capitals, and the bronze lamps suspended by chains, make the elegant structure a nostalgic vision of resuscitated antiquity.

Despite everything, Elizabeth returned to Corfu on several occasions. But Achilleion was put up for sale. "The thought of soon abandoning a spot moved me and made me love it, and thus each time I buried a dream too soon put to rest, I aspired to another which was not yet born."

On September 10, 1898, when Elizabeth left from the *Hotel Beau-Rivage* in Geneva to take an excursion on the lake to visit a Rothschild house nearby at Pregny, the Italian anarchist Luigi Luccheni stabbed her with a file. Thinking only that she was feeling ill, she was carried to the ship's upper bridge. When they discovered the wound, she was taken back to the hotel and died there, after they unlaced her bodice letting her bleed to death. Her last adventure would never take place.

During a repeat visit to Corfu in 1905, the beauty of the abandoned palace now moved the German emperor Wilhelm II (Elizabeth had sent him away in 1889 because she wanted no company while she was in mourning). He bought it two years later, changed the interior decoration, planted new, exotic things in the garden outside, and built a house of knights to accommodate his retinue. As a connoisseur of virile nudes, he preferred to replace the *Achilles Dying* with a triumphant hero. He therefore commissioned the sculptor Johannes Götz to create a colossal bronze statue of *Achilles Victorious*. During World War I, the French erased its martial inscription, "to the glory of German power," which he had put on the pedestal. In place of the temple that the empress had built for Heine, her favorite poet, he erected a monument to the creator of Achilleion, with her marble statue in the center.

The empress chose Corfu for her final residence. But imperial pomp had the last word for once, and her remains joined the crypt of the Capucine monks in Vienna, in the Habsburg tombs. The continent had ultimately captured the one who wanted "to make an island of herself."

Just as she fled reality by taking many cruises on the yacht *Miramar*, placed at her disposal by the Austrian fleet, Empress Elizabeth consoled her weary soul by incessant trips. Here the painter Wilhelm von Kaulbach depicts her during her last trip to Corfu in 1896.

The ceiling of Achilleion's vestibule is decorated with frescoes by the Italian Giuseppe Galloppi, dated 1891, representing *The Four Seasons* and *The Dance of the Hours*. Set in a rich frame of grotesques of Pompeiian inspiration, the fantasy of the figures that make merry among the foliage contrasts with the relative austerity of the fluted pilasters punctuating the vestibule.

PAGES 266–267: Achilleion's painted facades and vast terraces evoke the eclectic style of villas on the French Riviera. "I want a palace with colonnades and suspended gardens, one shielded from indiscrete gazes—a palace worthy of Achilles," the empress declared to Alexander von Warsberg, the distinguished Greek scholar to whom she entrusted the mission of giving form to her dream.

OVERLEAF: Entitled *Stella di Mare*, the chapel altarpiece painted by Franz Matsch portrays Elizabeth's vision in which the Virgin, protector of sailors, emerged from the waves. Elegantly proportioned, the apse above the Virgin has a painting by Mihail Munkacsy representing Christ before Pontius Pilate.

The grand staircase, in marble is framed by the guardian figures of Zeus and Hera: it is a veritable masterpiece. Smaller statues in the form of satyrs, water sprites and other mythological figures hold up the banister. These alternate with elegant supports where greenery unfolds. Stucco caryatids representing Apollo, Artemis, Aphrodite, and Hermes hold up the third-floor landing.

OVERLEAF: On the first landing, the stairway divides in two, then narrows into a single flight of stairs to the second landing, providing a lovely spatial effect.

Details of the banister of the staircase. Carefully cast and engraved, the figures which pretend to support the banister attest to the quality of decoration the empress desired.

OPPOSITE: Beneath the vault of the staircase, Franz Matsch painted *The Triumph of Achilles*. Following Homer's description in the Iliad, he portrayed the hero dragging the body of Hector around the ramparts of Troy on his chariot. The vault is decorated with architectural details inspired by paintings found at Pompeii and Herculaneum.

Supported by ionic columns, the Peristyle of Muses (also pages 278–279) is placed under the aegis of Apollo and the Nine Muses, daughters of Zeus and Mnemosyne. Some of these statues come from the Villa Borghese, while Empress Elizabeth commissioned others. The portico harbors a series of busts of philosophers, orators, and poets from antiquity.

OVERLEAF: Sculpted in marble by Ernst Gustav Herter, the statue of *Achilles Dying* once occupied the place of honor in the gardens of Achilleion. To this tragic vision of the hero, conforming to Elizabeth's sensibility, Wilhelm II preferred the effigy of the triumphant warrior, and relegated the marble statue to its current place behind the peristyle.

1 Palladianism is, loosely, a philosophy of design based on the writings and work of Andreas Palladio, an Italian architect of the sixteenth century who tried to recreate the style and proportions of the buildings of ancient Rome.

2 The Vallée aux Loups (Valley of Wolves) was François-René de Chateaubriand's estate. He was a preeminent early Romantic writer and poet.

3 The "lost illusions" reference is to Honoré de Balzac's famous novel *Les Illusions perdues* (*Lost Illusions*) written between 1835 and 1843.

4 The well-known phrase "enfants du siècle," translated as "children of the century," has come to indicate the malaise felt in the 1830s. It comes from Alfred de Musset's autobiographical *La Confession d'un enfant du siècle* and refers to the end of his love affair with George Sand.

5 Another well-known phrase "temps perdu" or "lost time" was coined from Marcel Proust's novel *A la recherche du temps perdu* (*A Remembrance of Things Past*). The author here again refers to Proust's novel when he speaks of Ludwig II of Bavaria as a very sensitive child, like the narrator in the novel. Proust published many novels between 1883 and 1903.

6 This reference is to the most famous scene from *Robert le Diable*, Giacomo Meyerbeer's opera, which opened in Paris in the early 1830s.

7 Mephistopheles, Faust, Marguerite. The reference is to the Faust legend, as it was done by Gounod in his opera, *Faust* (1859). The author refers to music later in the text when he discusses *Swan Lake* as a reference to the place where Ludwig II died (Starnberg Lake).

8 Positivism is a philosophy derived from the Romantic era. It is a system originated by Auguste Comte (1798–1857). It excludes from philosophy everything but the natural phenomena or properties of knowable things, together with their invariable relations of coexistence and succession, as occurring in time and space.

9 "Légende des siècles" refers to the epic poem by Victor Hugo (1802–1885).

10 The "Invitation au voyage" ("Invitation to the Voyage") is the title of a famous poem in *The Flowers of Evil*, by Charles Baudelaire, 1869.

11 *Les Trés Riches Heures du Duc de Berry* is the most famous book of hours, because it marks the zenith of manuscript illumination in late medieval Europe. It was made for the duc de Berry by the Limbourg brothers and is remarkable for the quality of its elegant miniatures.

12 "Castles in the air" is an English expression that refers to pipe dreams; the French phrase with the exact same meaning is "building castles in Spain."

13 Merlons are the solid part of an embattled parapet between two embrasures.

14 "Hotel des Invalides" refers to the famous lodging for retired soldiers in Paris. In 1670, Louis XIV—the Sun King—founded Les Invalides near what was then called the Grenelle Plain.

15 The ". . . like the frog in the fable . . ." is a reference to "La Grenouille qui veut se faire aussi grosse que le Boeuf" ("The Frog Who Wanted to Make Himself as Big as an Ox"), a famous fable by the seventeenth-century fabulist Jean de La Fontaine. In this fable, the frog puffed himself up till he burst.

16 The "gifts at the New Year" reference is to a French tradition in which families offer books as New Year's gifts to be read throughout the year.

17 Tristan and Isolde, and King Pepin and Berthe au Grand Pied are all famous medieval French legends. The legend of Tristan and Isolde (Tristram and Iseult) takes place during the Middle Ages, when knighthood and the chivalric code prevailed. Berthe au Grand Pied was the wife of King Pepin the Short; she was the mother of Charlemagne and

great-granddaughter of Charles Martel. Grand Pied translates to "large foot"; she was so named because of her club foot.

18 The allusion is to the famous description of Marcel Proust's "magic lantern." As a child Proust's narrator was given a kind of primitive projector, called a magic lantern, that allowed him to project images of his favorite medieval story characters onto his wall before going to sleep at night. These pictures seemed to move and dance when projected.

19 Bazar de la Charite was a once-popular marketplace in Paris, well known for the fire that claimed so many lives.

20 Armida and Rinaldo are the famous lovers from Tasso's epic poem *Jerusalem Delivered*.

21 Authari and Theodelinde is from the ancient Bavarian saga of Authari, king of Langobards, who wooed Princess Theodelinde, daughter of Garibald I.

22 Again, "remembrance of things past" is another reference to the novel by Marcel Proust (*see note 5*).

23 King Carol I's castle in the Carpathians is Peles Castle, which is discussed at length later in the text.

24 Rheinstein Castle was renamed Burg Rheinstein Castle after its rebuilding by Lassaulx.

25 Mayerling Affair. Crown Prince Rudolf and his seventeen-year-old mistress were either murdered or committed suicide at Mayerling.

26 King Jerome was the brother of Napoleon III, the archduke.

27 H.M. stands for His or Her Majesty (in this case Her), translated from S.M. (*Sire Majesté*) in French.

28 Book of hours (*see note 11*).

29 H.M. (*see note 27*).

30 "The cabbage, the goat, or the wolf" are mismatched guests of different social positions for whom there is a certain pecking order. A cabbage is eaten by a goat who in turn is eaten by a wolf. In other words, according to the queen, the groups of guests are not only very different, they are competitive with each other.

31 This story contains a sophisticated play on words. The gargoyle serves as a kind of pipeline (*conduit* in French, also meaning conduct or behavior) to remove unwanted rainwater from the roof. Because she is the king's mistress, the reference is both to her conduct and to the fact that her "plumbing system" is being used for the king's pleasure.

32 Gemeled windows are twin windows, placed side by side.

33 The writer has taken a famous soliloquy from *Phèdre* by Jean Racine, reworking it so that it reflects Ludwig II's state of mind.

34 *Boyar* is a member of a former privileged class in Romania.

35 Bougival and Trouville were fashionable French vacation spots that drew visitors of all kinds.

36 Caramania is a coastal town of Turkey, noted for its merchandising of Oriental rugs.

37 Edmond About, a well-known French writer, is trying via his anecdote, to explain the fact that here stark contrasts exist. His story involving the two hotels, one serving lunch and the other dinner, is his way of speaking to this contrast. In France, lunch is the main meal of the day, while dinner is a smaller meal; one is implicity more important than the other, even though they are both "meals." In Edmond About's account, the "authorities" had to intervene to make a fair exchange between the two hotels, because they were aware of the stark contrast—to them it was a fact that the difference was enormous, even though, on the surface, both hotels were equally benefiting. About does not underline the moral of this story (typical of French storytelling). This story speaks to the differences between the taste of the monarchs and the more colorful taste of the people; it speaks also to the composite of differing styles that appear in the castle, the different tastes that are mixed in one place.

INDEX

285

About, Edmond. *De Pontoise à Stamboul*. Paris: Librairie Hachette, 1884.

Bac, Ferdinand. *Le voyage romantique, Chez Louis II de Bavière*. Paris: Bibliothèque Charpentier, E. Fasquelle, 1910.

Bornheim, Werner, gen. Schilling. *Schloss Stolzenfels*. Mainz: Landesamt für Denkmalpflege, Burgen, Schlösser, Altertümer Rheinland-Pfaz, 1999.

Carneiro, Jose Martins, and Paulo Pereira. *Pena Palace*. London: Instituto Português do Patrimonio Arquitectonica and Scala Publishers, 1999.

D. Luis I. *Palacio Naconal da Ajuda*. Instituto Português do Patrimonio Arquitectonica, 1990.

Desing, Julius. *Königschloss Neuschwanstein*. Foto Studio Verlag Kienberger Gmbh, 1998.

Fabbiani, Rossella. *Anamnèses maximiliennes, Le château de Miramare*. In FMR n. 49, April 1994.

Fabbiani, Rossella. *Palazzo Miramare, Il Museo Storico* . Giulia: Electa/Ministero per i Beni e le Attività Culturali Soprintendenza per I Beni Ambientali Architettonici Archeologici Artistici e Storici del Friuli-Venezia, July 2001.

Flamburiari, S. L. *Corfu, the Garden Isle*. New York: John Murray in association with the Hellenic Group of Companies, Ltd., and Abbeville Press, 1994.

Haasen, Gisela. *Hohenschwangau, Vom Zauber eines romantischen Schlosses*. Munich: Bruckmann K. G., 1998.

Joanne, Adolphe. *Les bords du Rhin, illustrés*. Paris: Librairie-Hachette et Cie, 1863.

Lasdun, Susan, and Mark Girouard. *Victorians at Home*. London: Weidenfeld and Nicholson, 1981.

Le temps du voyage, voyage dans le temps,guide officiel établi par les Administrations des châteaux d'Allemagne. Schnell & Steiner, 1999.

McIntosh, Christopher. *The Swan King: Ludwig II of Bavaria*. New York: I. B. Tauris, 2003.

Merkle, Ludwig. *Ludwig II and His Dream Castles*. Munich: Stiebner Verlag, 2000.

----------. *Sissi, the Tragic Empress: The Story of Elisabeth of Austria*. Munich: F. Bruckmann Verlag & Druck Gmbh & Co.

Morand, Paul. *Voyages, "Bucarest."* Coll. Bouquins, R. Laffont, 2001.

Neumann, Dieter, and Rudolf Lehr. *Bad Ischl un die Habsburger*. Bad Ischl: Kurverband, 1992.

Orloff, Alexandre, and Dimitri Chvidkovsli. *Saint-Pétersbourg, l'architecture des tsars*. Paris: Mengès, 1995.

Popa, G., R. Rotarescu, R. Beldman, and M. Hortopan. *Castelului Peles, 125 de ani de la punera pietrei de temelie*. Muzeul National Peles, 1995.

Popa, Dan P., and Rodica Rotarescu. *Peles*. Sinaia: DEC et 2S Design, 1995.

ALEXANDRIA COTTAGE/PETERHOF PALACE
198516 Peterhof-St. Petersburg, Russia
Phone: (7) 812 4277425
Hours: 10:30 a.m.–6:00 p.m. (open daily May through October, except Mondays and the last Tuesday of the month); 11:00 a.m.–6:00 p.m. (November to May; open Saturdays and Sundays only)

HOHENSCHWANGAU CASTLE (Schloss Hohenschwangau)
Alpseestr. 24, D-87645 Hohenschwangau, Germany
Phone: (49) 8362 887198
Hours: 9:00 a.m.–6:00 p.m. (open daily April through September); 10:00 a.m.–4:00 p.m. (open daily October through March)

STOLZENFELS CASTLE (Schloss Stolzenfels)
56075 Koblenz, Germany
Phone: (49) 261 51656
Hours: 10:00 a.m.–6:00 p.m. (open daily Easter through September 30); 10:00 a.m.–5:00 p.m. (open daily October 1 through November 30; January 1 to Easter Sunday); Closed Mondays and during December

PENA PALACE (Palacio Nacional da Pena)
2710-609 Sintra, Portugal
Phone: (35) 219 105340
Hours: 10:00 a.m.–5:00 p.m. (open daily September 15 to June 15); 10:00 a.m.–7:00 p.m. (open daily June 15 to September 15); Closed Mondays

KAISERVILLA
A 4820 Bad Ischl, Austria
Phone: (43) 6132 23241
Hours: 9:00 a.m.–11:45 a.m./1:00 p.m.–4:45 p.m. (open daily May 1 through October 14)

MIRAMARE PALACE (Museo Storico del Castello di Miramare)
34014 Trieste, Italy
Phone: (39) 040 224143
Palace hours: 9:00 a.m.–7:00 p.m. (open daily)
Park tour hours: 8:00 a.m.–5:00 p.m. (daily November through February); 8:00 a.m.–6:00 p.m. (daily March through October); 8:00 a.m.–7:00 p.m. (daily April through September)

PIERREFONDS CASTLE (Château de Pierrefonds)
Rue Viollet-le-Duc, 60350 Pierrefonds, France
Phone: (33) 03 44427272
Hours: November through February: 10:00 a.m.–12:30 p.m. and 2:00 p.m.–5:00 p.m. (daily). March/April, September/October: 10:00 a.m.–12:30 p.m. and 2:00 p.m.–6:00 p.m. (Monday–Friday) and 10:00 a.m.–6:00 p.m. (Sundays); closed Saturdays. May/June: 10:00a.m.–6:00 p.m. (daily). July/August: 10:00 a.m.–6:00 p.m. (Monday–Saturday) and 10:00 a.m.–7:00 p.m. (Sundays)

AJUDA PALACE (Palacio Nacional da Ajuda)
Largo da Ajuda, 1300 Lisbon, Portugal
Phone: (351) 13637095
Hours: 10:00 a.m.–5:00 p.m. (daily); Closed Wednesdays and holidays

NEUSCHWANSTEIN CASTLE (Schloss Neuschwanstein)
87645 Schwangau, Germany
Phone: (49) 8362 939880
Hours: 9:00 a.m.–6:00 p.m. (daily April through September); 10:00 a.m.–4:00 p.m. (daily October through March)

PELES CASTLE (Muzeul National Peles)
2180 Sinaia, Str. Pelesului 2, Romania
Phone: (40) 244 312184
Hours: 10:00 a.m.–5:00 p.m. (daily); Closed Mondays

ACHILLEION VILLA (Achilleion Palace Museum)
Gastouri, Corfu, 49084, Greece
Phone: (30) 2661 056210
Hours: 8:00 a.m.–4:00 p.m. (daily)

ACKNOWLEDGMENTS

The authors and the editor wish to thank the curators and guides of the European castle-museums that opened their doors and archives, as well as the various organizations that authorized the photography. We are particularly grateful to the following:

Archduke Markus von Habsburg-Lorraine; José Mauel Marins Carneiro and Claude Pen (Pena Palace); Frau Kunze (Kaiservilla); Isabel da Silveira Godinho, Mari do Carmo Rebello de Andrade (Ajuda Palace), and the Instituto Português do Patrimonio Arqitectonico; Vadim Znamenov, Valentina Tenihina, Tatiana Khoroujaia, Elena Rogotnewa, and Igor Guerassimov (Peterhof Palace/Alexandria Cottage); Gabriela Popa, Liliana Manoliu, Mme. Rotarescu (Peles Castle).

We would also like to thank the following for their warm welcome: Rossella Fabbiani (Miramare Palace); Messeurs. Kritikos and Zadsoulis (Achilleion Palace); Herr Lange (Stolzenfels Castle) and the Garten und Schlossen von Rheinland Pfalz; M. Dejardins-Hayart, M. Brière, Mme. Lacroix, Mme. Outin, Mme. Legonidéc, and Mme. Lemire (Pierrefonds Castle), and the Centre des Monuments nationaux; Herr Luri, Mme. Pascale Bardou (Hohenschwangau Castle) and the Wittelsbach Fund; Herr Scheck (Neuschwanstein Castle) and the Garten und Schlossen von Bayern.

For help with the archival images and other documentation, we would to thank: Sylvie Aubenas, Jacqueline Martinet (Bibliothèque Nationale de France) and Sylvie Gabriel et Aldona Kucharska from the Hachette-Livre archives. And, finally, M. Holzenschuh, Cristina Gheaus, and Mme. Iliokratidou.

Jérôme Coignard personally thanks Claude d'Anthenaise, Agnès Carrayon, Emmauel Decaux, Gisèle Gachassin, Philip Mansel, and Bruno Villien.

Marc Walter would like to thank his father who assisted him in Bavaria and in Austria and his son Gaspard, who accompanied him to the banks of the Rhine. Finally, he would like to thank Mr. and Mrs. Fonda and their daughter who allowed him to take photos of Miramare Palace from aboard their boat.

PHOTO CREDITS

All of the photographs in this book are by Marc Walter, except for those belonging to the archives of the palaces or other sources, which are listed below.

ALEXANDRIA COTTAGE (The Peterhof Palace/Museum): pp. 18, 20, 21, 22 (left); HOHENSCHWANGAU CASTLE (Wittelsbach Ausgleichsfonds): pp. 38, 40, 41 (Herrenchiemsee Museum © Bayerische Verwaltung), 42 (right); STOLZENFELS CASTLE (Rheinland Pfalz): p. 65 (right); PENA PALACE (Instituto Portugues do Patrimonio Arquitectonico): pp. 92, 95 (center and right), 96, 97 (left), 111; KAISERVILLA: 116; MIRAMARE CASTLE (Ministero per i beni ed le attivita culturali): pp. 138, 139; AJUDA PALACE (Instituto Portugues do Patrimonio Arquitectonico): pp. 180, 182, 183, 184, 185; NEUSCHWANSTEIN CASTLE (Bayerische Verwaltung): pp. 210, 214; PELES CASTLE (Museu National Peles Sinaia): pp. 232 (right), 233 (left), 234; ACHILLEION VILLA: pp. 261, 262 (right), 263 (right), 265 (bottom). PHOTOTHÈQUE HACHETTE-LIVRE: pp. 42 (bottom), 63, 118, 132 (top), 163 (bottom), 231, 232 (left); SCHLOSS SCHÖNBRUNN: p. 127; MUSÉE NATIONAL DU CHÂTEAU DE VERSAILLES: p. 158; BIBLIOTHÈQUE NATIONALE DE FRANCE: p. 160 (left); BILDAGENTUR HUBER, Garmisch-Partenkirchen: pp. 208–209.

First published in the United States of America in 2004 by
The Vendome Press
1334 York Avenue
New York, NY 10021

Copyright © 2004 Éditions Gallimard
English translation copyright © 2004 The Vendome Press

ISBN: 0-86565-228-7

Library of Congress Cataloging-in-Publication Data

Coignard, Jérôme, 1957-
  [Palais romantiques. English]
  Dream palaces : the last royal courts of Europe / Jérôme Coignard, Marc Walter ; introduction by Archduke Markus Habsburg-Lorraine of Austria.
    p. cm.
  Includes bibliographical references and index.
  ISBN 0-86565-228-7 (alk. paper)
  1. Palaces--Europe. 2. Castles--Europe. 3. Architecture--Europe--19th century. 4. Europe--Kings and rulers--Dwellings. I. Walter, Marc. II. Title.
  NA7710.C6413 2004
  728.8'2'09409034--dc22
                                                    2004049604

Translated from the French by Karen Berrier

This volume was created by Studiochine for Gallimard Editions
Graphics: Marc Walter
Editorial assistance: Sabine Arqué
PAO (Desktop Publisher): Florence Cailly
Photoengraving: Ex-fabrica

Printed in China